Aunt Sally's Adirondack Kitchen

Most Requested Secret Recipes

by
Sally Longo
of
Aunt Sally's Catering

D1508900

Book design by Nancy Murtha
Cover Design by Christian Salmonsen
Photography by Gerry Lemmo, Sally Longo, Ben Moore, Ed Gazel
Foreword by Irv Dean

New York Press & Graphics
Albany, New York 12205
www.nypressandgraphics.com

First Edition, September 2007

First Printing, 2007

Copyright © Sally Longo 2007
www.adkcookbook.com

Printed in the United States of America

All rights reserved including the right to reproduce
this book, or parts thereof, in any form, except for
the inclusion of brief quotations in a review.

ISBN 978-1-60402-864-5

For Sara

THANK YOU

Thank you first and foremost, to all the people whose cooking inspired me: Grandma Dott, my mother Joan Gregory, Aunt Evelyn Meers, and the many family members and friends whose recipes are in my file box. Thank you, Sara, for being the best daughter I could ever have wished for and for proving that an 8 year old can work with filo dough! Thank you to my stepdaughter Amanda for letting me love her, for being so loving in return, and for teaching me how to make smoothies!

To my sister, Jacqueline Leto: I love you and pray for you in your daily struggle against chronic pain.

Extra special thanks to Nancy Murtha, whose work ethic and cheerful professionalism got this project in on time and made it seem easy. And we still managed to have great fun at our production meetings! Nancy designed and laid out the whole book except for the cover and managed to make sense of the scribbled recipes on scraps of paper that I handed to her. Nancy is the personification of the adage; "If you want something done, give it to a busy woman." and I am eternally grateful to her.

Much appreciation to Christian Salmonsen, who designed the cover, and to Gail Wilty, both of New York Press & Graphics.

Thank you to the thousands of catering clients, especially Mark Behan, who always wanted something a little different and inspired me to create new dishes.

Thanks to those who helped in ways both large and small: Irv Dean, Cindy Freed, June Carey, Susan McClanahan, Maureen Chase, Donna Slack, Judy Madison, Judy Johnson, Aileen Kane, Valerie Nusskern, Ed Gazel, and Lora Brody.

Many thanks to Melony Longhitano of A Lasting Impression Florist, who provided all of the beautiful arrangements in the photographs.

Big love to my nine nephews and niece, all of whom ask for their favorite dishes on their birthdays and special occasions. Of such stuff are the memories of a family made!

Table of Contents

Thank You
Foreword
Introduction
Aunt Sally's Favorite Kitchen Equipment

It's Finally Spring Celebration

You Say It's Your Birthday!

Elegant Bridal Shower Luncheon

Do-It-Yourself Graduation Barbecue

Father's Day Favorites

Lake George Summer Luncheon

Adirondack Hot Air Balloon Festival Party

Do-Ahead Cocktail Party

Après Cross-Country Skiing Party

Adirondack Christmas Cookie Swap

Make-Ahead Christmas Morning Brunch

Acknowledgements

Local Resources and Vendors

Index

Foreword

How, you might reasonably ask, does a grizzled, ink-stained journalist come to be pals with a popular caterer who has chosen to make the southern Adirondacks her niche?

The answer is quite simple. Sally Longo – "Aunt Sally" of Aunt Sally's Catering - was a fellow student a decade ago in a modern art history class, and we quickly discovered some mutual interests, a shared irreverence about - well, just about everything - and a passion for good food. Sally cemented what was to become an enduring friendship the day she brought wonderfully savory focaccia to class.

After the class had ended, we went our separate ways, I back to writing and editing for a living and eventually returning to my culinary connections by accepting an offer to write restaurant reviews for The Sunday Gazette of Schenectady, and Sally back to her catering business and her family.

Fast forward to a month ago, and Sally and I reunite over Mexican food. The conversation picks up where it left off. Some friendships are like that. We spoke of families, of work, and of course we talked about the state of food today.

Our objective in meeting was for me to get a look at Sally's work-in-progress, a cookbook, and I was eager to do so. I was not disappointed, though there was a part of me that wished that Sally's secret recipes could remain that way. (I don't, for example, tell anyone how I make my tarragon chicken salad or my Alsace-Lorraine specialty, choucroute.)

But, fellow foodies, Sally's benevolence is your good fortune. Besides the brilliant recipes she shares, there are Sally's wonderfully sprightly essays.

I could go on at length about what is contained in Sally's first cookbook - and I say "first," because it is my vision that this is but one of many cookbooks she will produce. But I'll keep it brief. Do not miss "Aunt Sally's Specialty Chicken", for it is genius in its simplicity. Her salmon dish with dill and leek sauce is a wonderful take on a classic. Then there are her "Pesto Pork Roast", her "Green Eggs and Ham" (what a terrific idea), and her accidental raspberry cream pound cake. There is so much more. Many of her recipes will make it into my culinary lexicon.

And just when you think it can't get any better, she offers us a holiday cookie section, a classic that might just become your Christmas baking bible.

The French have a wonderful saying about taste - chacun à son goût (each to his own). But, if you can't find something in Sally's cookbook that causes you to return to the kitchen, my advice is to have your taste buds checked.

Irv Dean
August 29, 2007

Catering

is not for sissies. I've done catering jobs in the blazing sun of a horse pasture and in below freezing temperatures of unheated garages. Running water and electricity are unexpected luxuries at many locations; let alone bathroom facilities. I've become an expert in makeshift kitchens and the porta-potty guys maintain a thriving business.

Many more variables come into play when catering an event in the Adirondack region. At a function I catered by the pond at the Adirondack Museum in Blue Mountain Lake, a museum staffer casually said to me, "You might want to cook facing the woods. We've had several visits from bears lately. At least you'd see them coming." I am not joking when I tell you I had a raw chunk of beef tenderloin ready to fling at an approaching bear, since I was also told that you can't escape a bear by running away.

In one forest setting, we had to station a person to shoo away a stealth chipmunk when we finally figured out why a Ziploc bag of freshly made croutons had holes chewed in it. As for ants, mosquitoes, and the infamous Adirondack black flies, you just have to grin and bear them.

There are many Adirondack Park regulations to consider. Most have no provisions for trash, and the rule is carry in-carry out. Many sites close at dusk, and the park ranger won't care if the bride is devastated about the wedding ending before she wants it to. Dumping dirty dishwater in any Adirondack Lake is definitely not allowed. Exhaustive planning is a must.

Then there is the weather to consider. Because of the mountains, you can't always see a stormy weather front approaching. Any Adirondack caterer will have a "suddenly the tent blew down right on top of the guests" story to tell! One caterer friend told me that after such a storm, she was plucking dinner napkins out of trees, and that a five-pound beef tenderloin blew right off a grill.

Tablecloth weights are standard equipment in my catering bag of tricks, and even then there are problems. Once some top heavy floral arrangements tipped over in a sudden gust of wind, and drenched the tablecloths an hour before the guests were due to arrive. We were in a field adjacent to Lake George. I sent the staff down to the lake to gather large pebbles, which we rinsed off and put in the bottoms of the vases. Then we blotted the tablecloths, laid them out in the sun, and had them back on the tables minutes before the guests arrived none the wiser.

Caterers are experts in crisis management. When a sudden storm, during which the rain blew sideways, deposited a river of mud right in front of the buffet table, I dispatched a staffer to a nearby hardware store to buy thirty feet of artificial grass runner, and the day was saved. Like an Adirondack duck, a caterer needs to glide smoothly on top of the water, while paddling like heck underneath.

It's no wonder that caterers are masters of do-ahead cooking; they need time for problem solving! The way that a caterer cooks is just right for the home cook, too. This book is full of delicious recipes that will give you a head start with your entertaining. You will learn how to get maximum flavor from minimal last minute fussing. Every recipe tells you how far ahead you can prepare it.

Cooking has always been my passion. Here in the foothills of the Adirondacks, it has been my good fortune to cater both to the locals with traditional tastes, and the more exotic palates of metropolitan tourists. The Adirondacks have a very long history of natives co-existing with rich and famous visitors. Thomas Jefferson, Teddy Roosevelt, and Georgia O'Keefe all came here and were moved to write about, paint, or protect our beautiful mountains and lakes. Tourists are as much a part of Adirondack history as the pivotal battles fought here during the Revolutionary War.

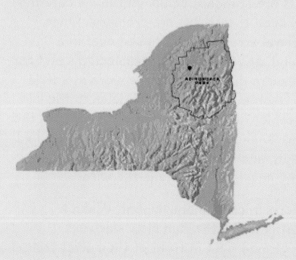

What is it like to live in the Adirondacks? The Adirondack Park spans six million acres: larger than Yellowstone, Everglades, Glacier and Grand Canyon National Parks combined. It is unique in that half of it is privately owned. The park contains over 2,300 lakes and ponds.

Most Adirondackers have some kind of connection to a lake. Whether they own a camp, have a boat, live full time on a lake, or know someone who does, most have had the experience of sitting in an Adirondack chair next to cone-laden arthritic looking pine trees and gently lapping waters with ducks paddling close by. Loons call out with a sound that perfectly describes whatever yearning lurks in your soul, yet you are happy.

I hope these recipes inspire you to cook,
and make you happy.

Aunt Sally's
Favorite Kitchen Equipment

Mandoline

Available in inexpensive plastic or pricy steel, these can slice, grate, and julienne anything in seconds. Once you try it, you'll love it. I actually prefer the plastic versions. Oriental stores sell them, also kitchen equipment stores.

Quick Tip Thermometer

Inexpensive and now available in most supermarkets, this type of thermometer is not left in the food during cooking. It gives an accurate reading within seconds and is a great way to test foods of varying densities, such as turkeys. Essential to ensure food safety and you only need one even if several dishes need testing.

Stick Blender

This is also known as an immersion blender. This is the very best way to puree soups and sauces without making a giant mess. It's handy for emulsifying salad dressings. Buy the best one you can afford; it will last longer.

Latte Frother

Sometimes I find these in the dollar store. They usually require 2 AAA batteries and the tiny round whisker at the end of it is great for whipping an egg for an egg wash.

Pie Bird

Usually available in the $10 range, this is a ceramic "bird" that is positioned in the center of the bottom pie crust before your fruit pie filling is mounded around it. Cut a small hole in your top crust to accommodate the bird, slipping the bird through the hole. Seal the crusts together as usual. When the pie is done, the juices will bubble up to the bird's mouth instead of escaping through the crimped crust. It's a great conversation piece.

Slow Cooker

Many recipes are easily adapted to the slow cooker. There isn't anything better than returning home from work and smelling that dinner is ready!

Wondra Quick-Mixing Flour

This super fine flour can be whisked directly into sauces and gravies, eliminating the need to make slurries or rouxs for thickening.

Baker's Joy Spray

A non-stick spray with flour which greases and flours your baking pans all at once. Need I say more?

Kitchen Bouquet/Gravy Master

This dark brown, roasted vegetable by-product gives anemic looking gravies a more appetizing color.

"In the spring,
at the end of the day,
one should smell like dirt."

~ Margaret Atwood

It's Finally Spring Celebration

Asparagus Cheddar Soup

Quinoa Pilaf

Spinach Feta Stuffed Chicken Breasts

Strawberry Rhubarb Pie

Fresh Fruit Pizza

Grandma Dott's Iced Tea

Winters

are long in the Adirondacks, which is why when spring finally arrives we are so appreciative of the wonderful things it brings. When the crocus and the grape hyacinths finally peek out, and the first fat robin lands on the lawn, it's time to start poking in the garden dirt to see if the ice is out. With a short growing season, it's common to have morning frost warnings well into May, so early gardening is a risky business. The first vase full of fresh flowers from my spring garden is always cause for celebration.

In the spring when asparagus is at its best and inexpensive, the **Asparagus Cheddar Soup** is an easy choice. You can prepare this soup days before serving it, but since it only takes about twenty minutes to make from start to finish, it's a good last minute recipe as well.

For those of you who haven't tried quinoa, you will be pleasantly surprised with the **Quinoa Pilaf**. This recipe is from Jim Murray, Executive Chef at the Glens Falls Hospital. Quinoa has been called the perfect grain, because ounce for ounce, it has the same amount of protein as meat and it is pleasantly chewy. Quinoa is now my favored pilaf grain, especially if there are vegetarians coming for dinner!

A simple, yet company-worthy, main dish is the **Spinach Feta Stuffed Chicken Breasts**. You can prepare the filling ahead of time, and refrigerate it until ready to assemble the dish. The roasting juices from the chicken are combined with heavy cream to make an unusually delicious sauce. Put the chicken on a platter and cover with foil while you are preparing the sauce. The chicken benefits from sitting and will be juicier than if it was served straight from the oven.

3

The **Fresh Fruit Pizza** can be made a day ahead. Experiment by using your favorite non-browning fresh fruits. This is a great recipe for kids to help with, and after tasting it, they will request it often. It's light and refreshing.

Rhubarb grows wild all over the Adirondacks. When we were kids, my friends and I would dare each other to eat it raw. I could never understand why people liked **Strawberry Rhubarb Pie**. This version is the result of several test runs. I added orange juice hoping it would lessen the tartness of the rhubarb. The juice made the pie watery, so the next time I threw in some grated orange rind instead. The final pie was really good, to my surprise.

Don't skip the step of letting the rhubarb sit in the sugar while you prepare everything else. This was an accident the first time. I had put the rhubarb and sugar in a bowl and I was interrupted by a long phone call before I had a chance to add the rest of the ingredients. When I returned, the rhubarb was sitting in sugary syrup. I drained the rhubarb, continued, and found that this mistake was a great improvement! Now Strawberry Rhubarb Pie is one of my favorites!

Grandma Dott's Iced Tea is named after my grandmother, Matilda. You'll never again be happy with instant iced teas after you try it. For me, the first sip of my grandmother's iced tea always summons the vision of her face. I use her yellow ceramic pitcher to this day.

So many family memories happen in the kitchen!

Asparagus Cheddar Soup

Serves 6

6 tablespoons **butter**
3/4 cup finely chopped **onion**
3/4 cup finely chopped **celery**
1/2 cup **flour**
6 cups **chicken broth**
1/4 cup dry **white wine**
1/8 teaspoon **Tabasco sauce**
1/8 teaspoon **Worcestershire sauce**
dash of **dry mustard**
1 pound trimmed **asparagus**, cut into 1/2" slices
8 ounces shredded **cheddar cheese**
2 teaspoons fresh chopped or 1/2 teaspoon dried **parsley**
1/4 teaspoon each, **salt** and **pepper**, or to taste
1 teaspoon **Wondra** quick-mixing flour

MELT the butter in a stockpot over medium heat.

ADD the onion and celery to the melted butter. Cook until tender, about five minutes.

WHISK the flour into the butter mixture, and cook for five minutes.

WHISK the chicken broth into the mixture, and bring to a boil.

REDUCE the heat.

ADD the wine, Tabasco sauce, Worcestershire sauce and dry mustard.

SIMMER for twenty minutes.

ADD the asparagus, and simmer ten minutes longer.

GRADUALLY whisk in the cheddar cheese and parsley to prevent the formation of lumps. Add salt and pepper to taste.

WHISK in the teaspoon of Wondra to keep the cheese from settling to the bottom.

COOK until the cheese is completely melted.

SEASON to taste with salt and pepper.

SERVE while hot.

Do-Ahead Tip: *This soup can be made two days in advance of serving.*

Quinoa Pilaf

Serves 6-8

4 cups **water** or **chicken broth**
1 12-ounce box of **quinoa**
2 peeled and diced **carrots**
1/2 cup sliced **scallions**
1/3 cup diced **celery**
1/2 **green pepper**, diced
1/2 **red pepper**, diced
1 cup sliced fresh **mushrooms**
1/4 cup minced fresh **parsley**
1 minced clove **garlic**
2 tablespoons **butter**
1 1/2 teaspoons **salt**
1/2 teaspoon **black pepper**

BRING the water or broth to a boil in a large saucepan.

ADD the remaining ingredients.

REDUCE the heat to low.

COVER and simmer until the quinoa is tender and the liquid has been absorbed, approximately 10-15 minutes.

STIR to fluff, and serve.

Do-Ahead Tip: The vegetables can be cut up the day before. Store, separately, in 'zip' bags. Refrigerate. This pilaf can be made one day in advance and reheated.

Spinach Feta
Stuffed Chicken Breasts

Serves 6

6 **chicken breast** halves, boned, skin left on
1 pound **fresh baby spinach**, washed
8 tablespoons **butter**
1 chopped medium **onion**
4 chopped **cloves garlic**
10 ounces crumbled **feta cheese**
1/4 teaspoon **nutmeg**
1/2 teaspoon each **salt** and **pepper**, or to taste
1 cup fresh **bread crumbs**
1/2 cup **heavy cream**
extra butter, softened
1/4 cup **white wine**
1 tablespoon **Wondra** quick-mixing flour
1 teaspoon **Kitchen Bouquet**, optional

PREHEAT the oven to 350 degrees.

SAUTE the onions and garlic in the butter until translucent.

ADD the baby spinach and sauté until just barely wilted.

PREPARE the bread crumbs by wadding fresh white bread slices into a firm ball and using a box grater to make the crumbs.

PUT the wilted spinach in a bowl, and add the feta, nutmeg, salt, pepper and the bread crumbs to make the stuffing.

MIX to combine.

CAREFULLY lift the skin of each chicken breast and put about 1/6th of the stuffing beneath it.

TUCK the skin and thin ends of the chicken under the breast to shape it into a mound.

USING fingers, coat the skin with a little soft butter.

PLACE the breasts in a greased metal 13"x9" roasting pan.

BAKE one hour, uncovered, or until the chicken tests done with a quick tip thermometer at 180 degrees.

REMOVE the breasts to a warm platter and loosely tent with foil.

HEAT the roasting pan on a stove burner.

ADD the white wine.

STIR to release the browned bits on the pan.

STRAIN the pan juices, saving only the liquid.

RETURN the strained juice to the roasting pan and simmer five minutes.

ADD the heavy cream and bring to a boil.

ADD any accumulated juices from the chicken platter.

WHISK in Wondra to thicken.

ADD some Kitchen Bouquet, if desired, to enhance the color of the gravy.

SIMMER five additional minutes.

SERVE the prepared gravy alongside the chicken breasts.

Do-Ahead Tip: *Make the stuffing the day before, and stuff the chicken just before baking.*

Spinach Feta Stuffed Chicken Breasts and Quinoa Pilaf

Strawberry Rhubarb Pie

Serves 6-8

2 rolled **pie crusts**
5 cups chopped **rhubarb**
1/4 cup sugar, plus 1/2 cup **sugar**
1 quart stemmed and halved **strawberries**
1 teaspoon **vanilla**
1/2 teaspoon **nutmeg**
2 tablespoons grated **orange peel**
1/4 cup **cornstarch**
4 tablespoons **butter**
1 **egg**
extra **sugar** for dusting
pie bird, optional

PREHEAT the oven to 400 degrees.

MIX 1/4 cup sugar and the rhubarb in a bowl and let sit while preparing the remainder of the pie. This draws off some of the rhubarb's tartness.

STIR the rhubarb occasionally.

MAKE a crust for a 2-crust pie or use purchased pie crusts. Line a 9" pie plate with one of the crusts.

PLACE the pie bird in the center, optional.

PUT the strawberries, vanilla, nutmeg, orange peel, cornstarch and 1/2 cup sugar into a bowl and stir together.

PREPARE the egg wash. In a small bowl, whip the egg using a latte frother while adding a tablespoon of water and beating well.

DRAIN the rhubarb; do not save the liquid.

MIX the rhubarb together with the strawberry mixture and pile into the bottom crust, evenly around the pie bird, if using.

CUT the butter into 4 pieces and scatter the pieces on top of the filling.

IF using the pie bird, cut a 1" hole in the center of the remaining pie crust with a cookie cutter or knife, and place the top crust onto the pie, slipping the hole carefully over the pie bird.

IF NOT using a pie bird, cut vents into the top crust.

CRIMP the edges as desired.

BRUSH the egg wash on top of the pie, and dust with the extra sugar.

BAKE 20 minutes.

REDUCE the oven temperature to 350 degrees.

BAKE 30 minutes longer, or until the crust is a deep golden brown.

Do-Ahead Tip: *This pie can be made one day in advance.*

Strawberry Rhubarb Pie using a pie bird

Fresh Fruit Pizza

Fresh Fruit Pizza

Serves 8

1 1/2 cups **flour**
3/4 cup **confectioner's sugar**
1/2 cup melted **butter**
8 ounces **cream cheese** at room temperature
1/2 cup **sour cream**
1/2 cup, plus 1/2 cup **sugar**
1/2 teaspoon **vanilla**
1 quart halved **strawberries** for the outside ring
2 sliced **mangoes** for the next ring
3 sliced **kiwi** for the next ring
1 pint **blackberries** for the center
1/2 cup **water**
1 teaspoon **lemon juice**
2 tablespoons **cornstarch**
1/2 cup **peach chardonnay**, or substitute apple juice or
     pineapple juice

PREHEAT the oven to 325 degrees.

COMBINE the flour, confectioner's sugar and melted butter to
make the crust, mixing with a fork until well blended.

PAT the crust mixture onto the bottom of a 12" inch pizza pan,
making a raised outer edge.

BAKE 15 minutes. Don't let the crust turn dark brown.

ALLOW the crust to cool.

TO prepare the filling, mix the cream cheese, sour cream, 1/2 cup
sugar and vanilla well with a hand mixer.

SPREAD the filling on top of the crust to the raised edge.

ARRANGE the fruit on top of the filling starting with the outer ring
of fruit, placing pieces of fruit closely together, completely
covering the cream cheese.

COMBINE the remaining 1/2 cup sugar, the water, lemon juice,
cornstarch and peach chardonnay in a saucepan.

STIR over high heat until the mixture comes to a full boil.

BOIL 30 seconds.

USING a pastry brush, paint the hot glaze over the tart, being
sure that all fruit is coated and any gaps are filled with glaze.

REFRIGERATE until ready to serve.

Do-Ahead Tip: *This "pizza" can be made the day before
serving.*

Grandma Dott's Iced Tea

Makes one gallon

1 gallon **water**
7 orange pekoe **tea bags**, tags removed
3 large **oranges**, juiced
3 **lemons**, juiced
1 cup **sugar**

BOIL the water in a large pot.

REMOVE from the heat and add the teabags.

LET sit undisturbed for an hour.

REMOVE the teabags.

ADD the sugar and fruit juices to the tea.

STIR until the sugar is dissolved.

TASTE for desired level of sweetness. Add more sugar to taste.

POUR the tea into two 2 quart pitchers.

REFRIGERATE until ready to drink.

Optional: When serving, add orange and lemon slices for garnish.

Do-Ahead Tip: This tea can be made several days in advance.

"Appreciate every moment
of every day
because in retrospect
they will all have gone by too fast."

~ M. Buchwald

You Say
It's Your
Birthday!

Spinach Salad with Poppy Seed Dressing

Oven Roasted Vegetables

Aunt Sally's Famous Specialty Chicken

Wedding Potatoes

Mango Martinis

Raspberry Whipped Cream Cake

Aunt Sally's Famous Specialty Chicken is

what I call a "Ripley" recipe; because of how it's made or what's in it, you just can't believe it could be any good. You would expect chicken breast that's been cooked twice to be tough, but you can eat this chicken with a cheap plastic fork and no knife at all; that's how tender it is! The cheese melts and combines with the chicken broth and with vigorous stirring, creates the delicious sauce that kept everyone guessing. I never expected it would become our most popular dish and people would beg for the recipe; some serious chefs and culinary arts graduates among them. This recipe pleases everyone, from fussy toddlers to gourmets.

As with so many of my recipes, the chicken can be prepared and assembled ahead of time, but don't add the broth until ready to bake. You can refrigerate or freeze it before baking - both methods give excellent results.

I have discovered that **Spinach Salad** is something most people don't think to make for themselves. The next time you have crisp bacon left over from breakfast, think about having spinach salad for dinner. Those bacon bits in a jar just don't cut it! Use baby spinach which is more delicate in flavor; you won't need to cut the stems off. The **Poppy Seed Dressing** is super easy, taking only a few minutes to whisk together. It can be made days ahead and refrigerated. Serve it on the side, so any leftover salad will keep until the next day.

The **Wedding Potatoes** are called that simply because I made them for my own wedding, which was also my first catering job! The wedding and reception took place at the home of my friends Mary Sue and Ron Raynor, and I got this recipe from Mary Sue. I hired a chef and a server, but I did all the prep cooking myself. That's when I first realized the importance of do-ahead recipes. Because catering my own wedding was so easy using this type of recipe, I found the courage to become a caterer.

Do try the **Oven Roasted Vegetables**. This cooking method brings out wonderful flavor in any vegetable. I once served oven roasted yellow squash to a friend and she exclaimed "I've never liked yellow squash, but this I could eat every day!" When I make a roasted vegetable medley, each vegetable is roasted on its own pan because carrots and other root vegetables take much longer to cook than tomatoes, squashes and similar vegetables.

Well, I confess! The **Raspberry Whipped Cream Cake** was born of desperation. Someone dropped a scratch cake right before a catering delivery. Frantic, I grabbed a box of the only cake mix on the shelf - pound cake! I made a two layer cake with canned raspberry pie filling in the middle and frosted it with sweetened whipped cream. I scattered fresh raspberries over the top and held my breath when it was served. It got rave reviews that time and every time since. So the moral of this story is that you should embrace your mistakes and accidents - very good things may come of them! After all, desperation IS the mother of invention....

When you are making the **Mango Martinis**, the secret to the success of this drink is using fully ripe mangoes. When unable to find ripe mangoes, I buy a quart carton of good quality mango puree from a local restaurant which stocks it at the bar. With your own sweet mangoes, or the purchased puree, this is so good that just one drink is very satisfying; but I always end up having two anyway!

Spinach Salad
with
Poppy Seed Dressing

Serves 8

2 bags pre-washed **baby spinach**
4 hard **boiled eggs**, peeled and sliced
1 16-ounce can **pitted black olives**, drained
1/2 small **red onion**, sliced paper thin
8 ounces sliced **fresh mushrooms**
1 pint **grape tomatoes**
    or 5 sliced **plum tomatoes**

RINSE the spinach and put it in a salad spinner to remove any excess water.

LAYER the ingredients in a pretty glass bowl, repeating the layers until all the ingredients have been used, and saving a small amount of each ingredient to arrange on the top.

SERVE with Poppy Seed Dressing (recipe follows) on the side so any leftover salad will keep for the next day.

Poppy Seed Dressing

1 cup **mayonnaise**
4 tablespoons **cider vinegar**
1/3 cup **sugar**
1/2 cup **whole milk**
2 tablespoons black **poppy seeds**
Pinch of **salt**

WHISK all the ingredients together in a bowl.

REFRIGERATE until ready to use.

Do-Ahead tip: The dressing can be prepared four days in advance.

Oven Roasted Vegetables

Serves 8 using the quantities listed
Roasting times are indicated in parentheses

1 **butternut squash**, cut into 1" cubes (35 minutes)
3 red **onions**, cut into 1" dice (30 minutes)
3 small **zucchini** or **yellow squash**, cut into 1" slices
    (45 minutes)
1 **eggplant**, peeled or not, cut into 1" slices (35 minutes)
1 **green bell pepper**, cut into 1" slices (20 minutes)
10 **plum tomatoes**, cut in quarters lengthwise, seeds
    and excess juice removed (30 minutes)
6 **carrots**, peeled and cut on the diagonal into 1/2"
    slices (25 minutes)
1 bunch **golden beets** (30 minutes)
1 bunch **asparagus**, cut in half crosswise (20 minutes)
olive oil
sea salt
freshly ground **black pepper**

PREHEAT the oven to 400 degrees.

PREPARE the vegetables as indicated.

SPREAD each vegetable on its own heavy baking sheet.

POUR a tablespoon of olive oil over each, and toss to evenly coat.

SPRINKLE with sea salt and pepper.

ROAST each baking sheet of vegetables for the time indicated
after each vegetable in the list of ingredients above.

CHECK them periodically - they are done when they begin to
shrink, are browned, and there is just a bit of blackening at the
edges.

COOL.

COMBINE the roasted vegetables.

SERVE or refrigerate.

Optional: *Pour one half cup hot water on the empty baking
sheet after roasting the vegetables and let it sit. Scrape the pan
with a rubber spatula when it is cool and pour off the juices. The
savory vegetable stock from this can be used in soup or stew.
This stock is also wonderful to use in place of plain water when
preparing taco meat or fajitas from a mix.*

Do-Ahead Tip: *The vegetables of choice can be prepared,
baked and combined two days in advance; then brought to room
temperature or reheated when ready to serve.*

Aunt Sally's Famous Specialty Chicken

Serves 6

3 pounds boneless, skinless **chicken breasts**, trimmed
3 **eggs**
1/2 teaspoon **salt**
1/2 teaspoon **pepper**
1/3 cup **Parmesan cheese**
2 cups unseasoned **bread crumbs**
2 14-1/2 ounce cans **chicken broth**
15 slices real **American cheese**
vegetable oil for frying

CUT the chicken breasts into 1/3" thick medallions, about 1 1/2" to 2" in diameter.

PUT the eggs, salt, pepper, and Parmesan cheese in a large bowl.

WHISK until well mixed.

ADD the chicken pieces, stirring to coat evenly.

REMOVE each chicken piece and dredge in the bread crumbs.

HEAT 1/4 inch vegetable oil in a shallow frying pan.

ADD the chicken pieces and fry until golden and completely cooked through.

REPEAT until all the chicken pieces have been fried.

MAKE a single layer of the cooked chicken in a 13"x9" pan.

COVER the chicken with a single layer of American cheese.

REPEAT. There will be two layers of chicken topped with two layers of cheese. *If not serving right away, cover and freeze or refrigerate at this point.*

WHEN ready to bake, preheat the oven to 350 degrees.

POUR the chicken broth over the top and cover with foil.

BAKE one hour. *If baking after being frozen, bake an hour and a half.*

REMOVE from the oven, uncover and stir to blend the cheese, chicken broth and chicken. Mix thoroughly for 2-3 minutes.

RETURN to the oven, uncovered, for ten minutes.

STIR once again, and serve.

Do-Ahead Tip: *This recipe can be prepared weeks in advance if being frozen, and three days in advance if refrigerated. Add the broth just prior to baking.*

**Wedding Potatoes, Aunt Sally's Famous Specialty Chicken, Mango Martinis
Raspberry Whipped Cream Cake, Oven Roasted Vegetables**

Wedding Potatoes

Serves 10-12

5 pounds **red bliss potatoes**, unpeeled, washed
1/2 cup **butter**
3 ounces **cream cheese**
1 cup **sour cream**
1/2 cup grated **sharp cheddar cheese**
1/2 cup **Parmesan cheese**
1/2 teaspoon **garlic powder,** or a few cloves of
    mashed roasted garlic
1 teaspoon each **salt** and **pepper** to taste

BOIL the potatoes until very tender, 45 minutes to one hour.
PREHEAT the oven to 350 degrees.
MASH the boiled potatoes by hand with a potato masher.
ADD the remaining ingredients.
STIR well.
PLACE the combined ingredients in a greased 4 quart casserole dish.
BAKE 30 minutes. *If refrigerated first, bake 45 minutes, or until hot in the center.*

Do-Ahead Tip: These potatoes can be prepared three days before baking and serving.

Mango Martinis

Serves 2

1/2 cup **orange juice**
1/2 cup **mango puree**
2 shots **Mandarin orange-flavored vodka**
1 cup **crushed ice**

PUT all the ingredients in a martini shaker.
SHAKE well.
STRAIN into two chilled martini glasses and serve immediately.

Do-Ahead Tip: Mango puree is available frozen or can be made by blending a ripe mango in the food processor with 1/4 cup orange juice.

Raspberry Whipped Cream Cake

Serves 10

1 box **pound cake mix**
1 can **raspberry pie filling**
1 quart **heavy cream**, divided
2/3 cup **confectioner's sugar**, divided
1 pint **fresh raspberries**

PREHEAT the oven to 350 degrees.

PREPARE the cake per package directions.

POUR the prepared pound cake mix into two greased and floured 9" round cake pans.

BAKE 18-20 minutes or until a toothpick inserted in the centers of the cakes comes out clean.

COOL the cakes and remove from the pans.

PLACE one cake on a serving plate, upside down.

SPREAD 3/4 of a can of raspberry pie filling, keeping it toward the middle as it will spread more when the second layer is added.

POSITION the top layer right side up without applying any pressure.

IN a mixing bowl, beat 2 cups of the heavy cream for a minute.

ADD 1/3 cup confectioner's sugar and continue beating until the cream is very stiff and yellowish streaks begin to appear.

FROST the cake with the whipped cream.

TO pipe decorative borders, whip the remaining two cups of cream with the remaining 1/3 cup confectioner's sugar.

PIPE a large circle in the center of the cake and fill it with the remaining 1/4 can of the pie filling.

USE the remainder of whipped frosting to pipe decorative borders around the rest of the cake.

ADD the fresh raspberries on top of the pie filling.

REFRIGERATE until ready to serve.

Do-Ahead Tip: *This cake can be made a day in advance.*

"In all of the wedding cake,
hope is the sweetest of plums."

~ Douglas Jerrold

Elegant Bridal Shower Luncheon

English Cucumber Canapés

Almond Stuffed Bacon Wrapped Dates

Spring Mix Salad with Gorgonzola, Spiced Pecans,
Red Pears and
Aunt Sally's Famous Balsamic Vinaigrette

Herb Encrusted Salmon with Dill Leek Sauce

Slow Cooker Bananas Foster

Lemon Diamonds

Kir Royales

A bridal

shower is always a happy occasion, as large groups of women never fail to have a good time. This menu always leaves everyone content and happy to sit through three hours of gift opening.

The **English Cucumber Canapés** are simple and refreshing, offering a nice contrast to the **Almond Stuffed Bacon Wrapped Dates**. You can marinate the cucumbers five days in advance and even cut out the bread circles two or three days ahead of time. Assembly will only take a few minutes on the day of the shower. The Almond Stuffed Bacon Wrapped Dates incorporate the savory crispness of bacon with the warm sweetness of dates. The almond adds crunch, with the result being a surefire conversation starter. I always try to include one recipe in every menu that has a touch of a surprise and will get people talking.

You'll see many versions of the **Spring Mix Salad** recipe in restaurants, and it is delicious. If you have lots of people coming, call a local produce wholesaler to see if they will sell you a three pound box of the spring mix. It will be fresher and much less expensive than what you can buy in the market. The **Spiced Pecans** can be made weeks ahead of time, except that you'll probably eat them before the party! A jar of these pecans makes a great holiday gift. Many people asked me to market them, but I'm giving you the recipe instead.

Aunt Sally's Famous Balsamic Vinaigrette is one of my top five requested recipes. Isn't it nice that it starts with a mix, is easy to prepare, and keeps for two weeks in the refrigerator? If you don't have a stick blender, you should get one, as it aerates the dressing and lightens the color from dark brown to light caramel.

Lake George is renowned for its fishing as the lake is home to landlocked salmon, pike, and several kinds of trout and bass. If you don't have a fisherman in your family, buy Alaskan salmon for the showstopper **Herb Encrusted Salmon** dish. It was my most popular fish entree from day one. Both the **Dill Leek Sauce** and the herbed bread crumb topping can be prepared days ahead of time and refrigerated, or even frozen until ready to use. The Dill Leek Sauce is really delicious - one of my friends used to eat it like soup. As with so many good recipes, it is simple, with few ingredients.

There are many versions of **Lemon Diamonds**. For this version, I combined four different recipes and tinkered until it was the best one I had ever tasted. The coconut doesn't announce itself but lends a wonderful moistness and chewiness. My catering help fights over leftover Lemon Diamonds; that is, if there ever are any.

If you don't have time to make the Lemon Diamonds, serve the **Slow Cooker Bananas Foster**. Using a slow cooker makes this dessert ridiculously easy, and it is so delicious that it generally leaves people speechless after the first spoonful.

A final surprise awaits if you've never had a **Kir Royale**. You will love having something so simple in your repertoire that announces - "This is an occasion to be remembered".

English Cucumber Canapés

Makes 36

1 peeled **English cucumber**, sliced into very thin circles
    with a mandoline
1 small **onion**, sliced
1 10-ounce bottle **white balsamic vinegar** – as this is
    the key to the wonderful flavor, no substitutions
1 sliced **loaf rye or pumpernickel bread**
Hellmann's **mayonnaise**
10 pitted **black olives**, sliced in thin rings

PLACE the cucumber slices in a small deep glass dish.

STIR in the onions and vinegar.

COVER with plastic wrap and refrigerate until ready to use. The cucumber slices need at least a day to marinate.

CUT the loaf of rye, or pumpernickel, bread into small crustless circles using a round cutter about the same diameter as the cucumber slices.

WHEN ready to make the canapés, spread a thin coating of mayonnaise on each bread circle.

REMOVE the number of cucumber slices equal to the number of bread circles being used, and drain for a few minutes in a colander. The onions do not get used in the canapés.

PLACE one cucumber circle on each circle of prepared bread, and top with an olive slice.

COVER with plastic wrap and refrigerate until ready to serve.

Do-Ahead Tip: *The cucumbers can be made and refrigerated five days in advance. The bread circles can be cut, and then stored for up to three days in advance. Complete assembly can be done two hours ahead. Cover and refrigerate.*

Almond Stuffed
Bacon Wrapped Dates

Makes 36

36 whole **dates**, pitted
36 whole **almonds**
36 slices **pre-cooked or uncooked bacon**

IF using uncooked bacon, fry the slices to a pre-crisp stage.

DRAIN the partially cooked bacon on paper towels.

STUFF each date with an almond.

WRAP the stuffed date in a slice of the bacon, and secure with a wooden toothpick.

PLACE them on a broiler pan and broil on high until the bacon is browned and crispy. If the bacon has not browned on both sides, turn the dates over and return to the oven until crispy.

REMOVE to a paper towel to cool for a minute or two.

SERVE immediately.

Optional: *Lightly sprinkle brown sugar over the dates before they go in the oven if a sweeter taste is preferred.*

Do-Ahead Tip: *These can be assembled two days in advance and stored in the refrigerator until ready to broil.*

English Cucumber Canapés and Almond Stuffed Bacon Wrapped Dates

Spring Mix Salad with Gorgonzola, Spiced Pecans, Red Pears and Aunt Sally's Famous Balsamic Vinaigrette

Serves 6

1/2 pound **spring mix salad**
2 ripe **red pears**, unpeeled and cored
spiced pecans (recipe follows)
5-6 ounces **gorgonzola** or **blue cheese**
balsamic vinaigrette (recipe follows)

DIVIDE the spring mix onto six salad plates.

DIVIDE the gorgonzola evenly and add about eight spiced pecans per plate.

DICE the pears and divide among the plates.

TOP with balsamic vinaigrette, or put it in a small pitcher to pass.

Do-Ahead Tip: *Place the spring mix salad on individual plates up to three hours in advance. Cover with plastic wrap and refrigerate, adding the pears right before serving.*

Spiced Pecans

1 **egg white**
2 tablespoons **water**
1/8 teaspoon **cloves**
1/4 teaspoon **cinnamon**
1/4 teaspoon **allspice**
1/2 teaspoon **cayenne**, or to taste
1/2 teaspoon **salt**
4 cups **whole pecan halves**
1/2 cup **sugar**

PREHEAT the oven to 250 degrees.

COAT a large cookie sheet with baking spray.

WHISK together all the ingredients **except** the pecans and sugar.

LET the mixture rest for 15 minutes.

ADD the pecans to the mixture, tossing to coat.

29

ADD the sugar, working quickly to mix well but not waiting until the sugar dissolves.

TURN the pecans out onto the cookie sheet in a single layer.

BAKE one hour.

COOL for two minutes.

USING a metal spatula, loosen the pecans.

COOL completely on the cookie sheet before storing in an air tight container.

Do-Ahead Tip: *These pecans can be made a month in advance.*

Aunt Sally's Famous Balsamic Vinaigrette

1 package **Good Season's Italian Dressing**
1/4 cup **Balsamic vinegar**
1/2 cup **vegetable oil**
3 tablespoons **water**
1/8 cup **Parmesan cheese**

COMBINE the ingredients and mix thoroughly.

STORE the dressing in the refrigerator.

Tip: *Excellent results are achieved by mixing with a stick blender. This adds air and lightens the color of the dressing, although a hand mixer will result in a similar outcome.*

Do-Ahead Tip: *The vinaigrette can be made two weeks in advance and refrigerated.*

Herb Encrusted Salmon
with
Dill Leek Sauce

Serves 4-6

750 ml bottle **dry white vermouth**
2 cups sliced **leeks**, white parts only (supplement with
    onions if needed)
1 quart **heavy cream**
1 tablespoon, plus 2 teaspoons **dried dill**
1 tablespoon **horseradish**, or to taste
1/2 cup melted **butter**
4 cups **fresh white breadcrumbs**
2 tablespoons **butter**
2 tablespoons **oil**
1 clove **minced garlic**
1/2 cup chopped **onion**
1 pound **fresh baby spinach**, washed
2 pounds boned **salmon fillets**
Wondra quick-mixing flour, optional

Sauce

BRING the white vermouth and sliced leeks to a boil until the
liquid is reduced to about 1/4 cup.

ADD the cream and 1 tablespoon dried dill.

BOIL until slightly thickened, adding Wondra if desired.

SET aside.

Bread Crumb Topping

PREPARE the bread crumbs by wadding fresh white bread slices
into a firm ball and using a box grater to make the crumbs.

PUT the crumbs into a mixing bowl.

WHISK together the remaining two teaspoons dried dill, the
horseradish and 1/2 cup melted butter in a small mixing bowl.

POUR the butter mixture over the bread crumbs and stir
vigorously until well combined.

Wilted Spinach

IN a large sauce pan, melt two tablespoons butter, adding the oil, onion and garlic; cooking on medium heat until onions are translucent.

ADD half of the baby spinach, and toss just until wilted.

ADD the remaining half of the spinach, continuing to toss until wilted.

SET aside.

Salmon

PREHEAT the oven to 375 degrees.

PLACE the salmon fillets, skin side down, on a baking sheet lined with foil, shiny side up. Don't grease the foil. The skin will stick to the foil while baking, creating an easy way to remove the skin.

EVENLY divide bread crumb topping on the fish fillets, pressing down slightly.

BAKE the fish 15 minutes, or until a toothpick slides in and out easily.

Serving

REHEAT the sauce if necessary.

FORM a ring of the wilted spinach on each individual dinner plate.

FILL the hole with some dill leek sauce.

PLACE a serving size portion of salmon on top of the sauce.

Do-Ahead Tip: The sauce and the crumbs can be made three days in advance and refrigerated. If frozen, they can be made a month in advance. Bring both to room temperature before using. The bread crumb topping can be put on the salmon in the morning, and then refrigerated until ready to bake.

Herb Encrusted Salmon with Dill Leek Sauce
on Wilted Spinach

Slow Cooker Bananas Foster

Serves 12

1 cup **butter**
1 cup **light brown sugar**
1/2 cup **Captain Morgan's Spiced Rum**, no
    substitutions!
2 teaspoons **corn starch**, optional
1/2 gallon **vanilla ice cream**
12 **bananas**

COMBINE the butter, brown sugar and rum in a slow cooker at least three hours before planning to serve this dessert.

STIR to dissolve the sugar a bit.

COOK on low for approximately three to six hours.

WHISK vigorously three or four times during the cooking period. Don't be concerned if foaming occurs. If the mixture appears to have separated, whisk until it comes together once again.

THICKEN with corn starch, if desired.

LADLE some sauce over a big scoop of vanilla ice cream and top with a sliced banana.

Optional: For an even richer flavor, slice the bananas right into the hot sauce, heating them for five minutes before serving with the ice cream.

Do-Ahead Tip: The sauce can be made a week in advance and refrigerated. Simply reheat before serving.

Slow Cooker Bananas Foster

Lemon Diamonds

Makes 24

2 cups, plus 2 teaspoons **flour**
1/2 cup, plus 1 1/2 cups **sugar**
1/2 teaspoon, plus a pinch of **salt**
1 1/2 cups **coconut**
12 tablespoons cold **butter**
4 **eggs**
1/2 cup fresh **lemon juice**
2 tablespoons grated **lemon peel**
1 teaspoon **baking powder**
1/2 cup **confectioner's sugar**

PREHEAT the oven to 350 degrees.

LINE a 13"x9" baking pan with foil, the shiny side up. Butter the foil.

PREPARE the crust by combining two cups flour, 1/2 cup sugar, 1/2 teaspoon salt and the coconut in a food processor. Follow with a few quick pulses to mix the ingredients.

CUT the cold butter into cubes and add to the food processor. Pulse until uniformly mixed, stopping before a ball of dough forms.

PRESS the dough evenly over the bottom of the baking pan.

BAKE 25 minutes until the crust is golden at the edges.

WHILE the crust is baking, put 1 1/2 cups sugar, 4 eggs, the lemon juice, lemon peel, two teaspoons flour, baking powder and pinch of salt into the previously used, unwashed, food processor and blend until smooth.

REMOVE the crust from the oven when done and pour the filling over it.

RETURN to the oven and bake 30 minutes. The filling will be browning at the edges when done.

REMOVE and cool completely. Dust the top with confectioner's sugar.

LIFT out of the pan by carefully pulling on the foil. Peel the foil back and cut into bars.

Do-Ahead Tip: *These bars can be made five days in advance.*

Kir Royales

Serves 6

one bottle of a **favorite champagne**
one bottle **crème de cassis**

MEASURE and pour 1 tablespoon of the crè me de cassis into each champagne glass.

FILL the remainder of the glass with champagne.

SERVE immediately.

Kir Royales and Lemon Diamonds

"There is a good reason
they call these ceremonies
'commencement exercises'.
Graduation is not the end,
it's the beginning."

~ Orrin Hatch

Do-It-Yourself Graduation Barbecue

Grilled Chicken with Scallion Drizzle

Slow Cooker Pulled Pork

Oriental Pasta Salad

Mediterranean Orzo Salad

Lobster Broccoli Pasta Salad

Red Bliss Potato Salad

Country Baked Beans

"Not Flat" Chocolate Chip Cookies

Scratch Lemonade

When a mother of the bride tells me she wants to self-cater a post wedding brunch, I always talk her out of it. When a mother says she wants to self-cater her child's graduation party, I tell her that's very do-able. Here's a menu that any good home cook can manage. I have included more salads than are necessary so that you can select the ones that appeal to you. Every single dish can be prepared days ahead of time, except for the actual grilling of the chicken. And if you're lucky, you'll have a volunteer to man the grill!

Using boneless chicken tenderloins or thighs for the **Grilled Chicken with Scallion Drizzle** means a shorter cooking time and also maximizes your grill space. The Scallion Drizzle gives the chicken a great flavor boost.

An interesting thing happened when I started doing the local TV cooking show. I noticed right away that the recipes the viewers wanted were not the labor intensive, haute gourmet ones. They wanted the "it's quick, easy, tasty and it gets dinner on the table" recipes. The **Slow Cooker Pulled Pork** recipe is one of those and it couldn't be easier – I think you'll agree.

Ugh - potato salad. This simple dish used to scare me. So many variables! Boil the potatoes whole or chopped? Peeled or unpeeled? How do you tell when they're done? Should you marinate the hot potatoes in a vinaigrette? Add onions? Hard boiled eggs? One day, frustrated with a bland batch of potato salad, I picked up a canister of ranch dressing powdered mix and dumped a ridiculous amount of it into the bowl. The **Red Bliss Potato Salad** was fantastic! People always ask what the secret ingredient is. In my early days, I sneered at using prepared products, but if they give a delicious result, why not? The method of cooking the potatoes was discovered by my sister Gail. She had overcooked red potatoes for a potato salad to the point that they were mash-able. She was so upset, she threw the drained potatoes into the refrigerator, decided to deal with them the next day and went to bed. To her surprise, the next morning the potatoes had firmed up and were perfect for potato salad!

There is a lot of guessing about the secret ingredients in the **Country Baked Beans**. I add kielbasa instead of the usual bacon and also some chopped chipotle chiles. The chiles add a wonderful smokiness, heat, and richness of flavor.

The other salads were selected for this book because they're a little something different. I think you'll love each one. The **Mediterranean Orzo Salad** was inspired by one of my favorite cookbook authors, Ina Garten. Her recipes are deceptively simple and completely delicious.

The **"Not Flat" Chocolate Chip Cookie** recipe is the result of much experimentation. I needed a cookie that could be shipped, without breaking, to my stepdaughter Amanda at college. Later, we served them at a party and everyone wanted to know how we made chocolate chip cookies that weren't flat. Hence the name...

The **Scratch Lemonade** calls for a simple sugar syrup. Believe me, this recipe is worth doing. It's also a great conversation starter. Explain to your guests how to mix it to their idea of perfect sweetness and walk away. They'll be chatting and laughing in no time!

Grilled Chicken
with
Scallion Drizzle

Serves 6

2 pounds **chicken breasts**, cut into slices no more
     than 1/2" thick OR 2 pounds **chicken breast
     tenderloins**
1 cup sliced **scallions**
1/2 cup **olive oil**
1 1/2 teaspoons sea **salt**
1 teaspoon **black pepper**
ten large **fresh basil leaves**, sliced
3 small or one large clove **garlic**

PLACE all the ingredients, **except** the chicken, in a food processor
to make the drizzle.

PROCESS until well blended and uniform in texture.

DIVIDE the drizzle into two equal portions.

PUT one half of the drizzle in a large 'zip' bag.

ADD the chicken to the 'zip' bag.

TURN the chicken in the drizzle to thoroughly coat the chicken.

REFRIGERATE the marinating chicken overnight along with the
remaining half of the scallion drizzle.

GRILL the chicken, discarding the drizzle marinade.

TOP the grilled chicken with the reserved drizzle just before
serving it.

Optional: Boneless
chicken thighs or raw,
peeled shrimp can be
substituted for the
chicken breasts.

Do-Ahead Tip:
Marinate the chicken
the day before. Grill
just before serving.
The scallion drizzle can
be prepared two days in
advance and then
refrigerated.

Slow Cooker Pulled Pork

Serves 6-8

2 pounds **boneless country style pork spareribs**,
   trimmed of excess fat
1 sliced **onion**
1 16-ounce bottle **barbecue sauce**
8 **sandwich rolls**

PLACE the trimmed pork and onion in a slow cooker.

POUR the barbecue sauce into the slow cooker.

COOK on low 8-10 hours. Do not remove the lid of the slow cooker or stir during this time.

WHEN ready to serve, stir vigorously until the pork falls apart and is thoroughly mixed with the barbecue sauce and onion.

SERVE with warmed, split rolls.

Do-Ahead Tip: *The pulled pork can be made three days in advance and reheated on low in the slow cooker.*

Oriental Pasta Salad

Serves 12

1 pound cavatappi **pasta**
8 ounces **sugar snap peas**, raw and cut in half crosswise
    (fresh snow peas will also work)
4 sliced **scallions**
2 stalks **celery**, thinly sliced on the diagonal
3 **carrots**, peeled and julienned on a mandoline
1 can whole water **chestnuts**, rinsed, drained and cut
    into halves
1 medium **jicama**, peeled, and julienned on a mandoline
1 cup sliced **grilled chicken**, optional
1/3 cup **peanut satay sauce** (recipe follows) or use
    bottled Bangkok Padang Peanut Sauce
1/3 cup rinsed **peanuts**, optional
1/2 teaspoon **red pepper flakes**, optional
1 cup Hellmann's **mayonnaise**, or to taste
1/4 teaspoon each **salt** and **pepper**, or to taste
1/4 cup chopped fresh **cilantro**. optional

COOK the pasta to al dente in salted boiling water, rinsing with cold water to halt the cooking process.
DRAIN well.
ADD the remaining ingredients.
IF serving right away, stir in additional mayonnaise to achieve the desired level of moistness. If serving hours later or the next day, wait until just before serving to adjust the mayonnaise, as the pasta will absorb it.
GARNISH with the chopped cilantro, if desired.

Peanut Satay Sauce

1 cup **chunky peanut butter**
1/2 cup **chicken broth** OR coconut milk
2 tablespoons unseasoned **rice wine**
2 tablespoons low sodium **soy sauce**
1 tablespoon Thai **hot chili sauce**, to taste
1 tablespoon **fish sauce** (nam pla)
1/4 cup **light brown sugar**
1" chunk **ginger**, peeled and grated
2 cloves **garlic**, minced or grated
1/2 teaspoon **cayenne pepper**

PLACE all the ingredients in a blender or food processor and pulse until sauce is uniform and thoroughly blended.

ADD more chicken broth or coconut milk for a thinner sauce.

REFRIGERATE.

Do-Ahead Tip: The peanut sauce can be made three days in advance. The salad can be made two days in advance. Check before serving to see if more mayonnaise is needed before serving.

Mediterranean Orzo Salad

Mediterranean Orzo Salad

Serves 12

Vegetable Preparation

2 small **white eggplants**, peeled and cubed (white
    eggplant is less likely to be bitter)
2 small **yellow squash**, halved, seeds scraped out,
    sliced 1" thick
2 small **zucchini**, halved, seeds scraped out, sliced 1"
    thick
1 basket **cherry tomatoes**, halved, seeds removed
1 large or two small **red onions**, cut into 1" dice
1 **red bell pepper**, cut into 1" dice
1 **orange (or yellow) bell pepper**, cut into 1" dice
olive oil
sea salt or kosher salt
freshly ground **black pepper**

PREHEAT the oven to 425 degrees.

PLACE vegetables in a single layer, using multiple baking sheets if
necessary.

DRIZZLE each pan of vegetables with one tablespoon olive oil,
and sprinkle with the salt and pepper.

TOSS to coat all the vegetables right on the baking sheets.

BAKE approximately 25 minutes until definite caramelizing occurs.
The vegetables will seem right on the edge of burning when done.

LET the vegetables cool on the baking sheets.

PUT the vegetables into a large bowl.

Dressing

1/3 cup freshly squeezed **lemon juice**
1/3 cup **olive oil**
1 teaspoon kosher or **sea salt**
1/2 teaspoon freshly ground **black pepper**

WHISK all ingredients vigorously together.

SET aside while cooking the orzo.

Orzo

1 pound **orzo**
1 teaspoon **salt**

ADD the orzo to rapidly boiling salted water and cook no longer than eight minutes. It may not appear to be done, but will continue to swell as it cools.

DRAIN well. Do not rinse with cold water as leaving the starchy coating on the cooked orzo will help the dressing stick to it.

ADD the cooked orzo to the cooled vegetables.

STIR in the dressing and mix well.

Extras - Optional

1/2 cup crumbled **feta cheese**
2 thinly sliced **scallions**
1/4 cup toasted **pignolas**
1/2 cup pitted **kalamata olives**, halved
5 large or 10 small **fresh basil leaves**, thinly sliced
1/4 teaspoon each **salt** and **pepper**, or to taste

FOLD any or all of the optional ingredients into the prepared orzo salad.

REFRIGERATE until ready to serve.

TASTE for seasonings. This salad requires adequate salt. If it does not seem really delicious, add more salt and pepper.

ALLOW the salad to come to room temperature before serving. The flavors will be more intense.

Do-Ahead Tip: The roasted vegetables and the dressing can be prepared four days in advance and stored in the refrigerator. The entire salad can be made two days in advance.

Mediterranean Orzo Salad
Slow Cooker Pulled Pork on rolls
Country Baked Beans
Grilled Chicken with Scallion Drizzle

Lobster Broccoli Pasta Salad

Serves 10

1 cup Hellmann's **mayonnaise**
1 cup **sour cream**
1 package **Good Seasons Cheese Garlic Dressing**
  (or substitute a favorite Good Seasons mix)
2 tablespoons dried **dill weed**
2 tablespoons **lemon juice**
1 pound **radiatore pasta**
1 large head **broccoli**
2 pounds frozen cooked **lobster meat** OR one pound
  cooked lobster and one pound cooked large shrimp

COMBINE the mayonnaise, sour cream, dressing mix, dill weed and lemon juice in a bowl to make the dressing.

MIX well, and put the dressing in the refrigerator until ready to proceed.

PREPARE the pasta per package directions, cooked al dente, drained and cooled.

CUT the broccoli into florets and steam over boiling water for three minutes. Run cold water over the broccoli to halt the cooking process.

THAW the pre-cooked lobster meat and/or shrimp. Break large chunks of lobster into bite sized pieces, checking for and removing shell fragments and cartilage.

SET aside a handful of lobster pieces and broccoli florets, and refrigerate.

COMBINE the pasta, broccoli, lobster (and shrimp) in a large bowl with 1 1/2 cups of the dressing.

STIR well to coat all the ingredients evenly.

REFRIGERATE the salad until ready to serve.

ADD more dressing to adjust the moistness of the salad to taste.

TOP with the reserved lobster pieces and broccoli florets before serving.

Do-Ahead Tip: The dressing can be made five days in advance and the broccoli can be steamed three days ahead of time. The salad can be made a day in advance.

Red Bliss Potato Salad

Serves 12

5 pounds unpeeled **red bliss potatoes**
4 stalks diced **celery**
1 tablespoon very finely minced **sweet onion**
6 chopped hard **boiled eggs**
1/2 cup sliced **green stuffed olives**, optional
1/3 cup **Hidden Valley Ranch Dressing** powdered mix
2 cups Hellmann's **mayonnaise**, or to taste
1 teaspoon **salt**
1/2 teaspoon **pepper**

PLACE the scrubbed potatoes in a large stockpot. Be sure the potatoes are at least two inches under water.

SALT the water, and bring to a boil.

TEST the potatoes for doneness after 20 minutes.

BOIL until potatoes test done. When the potatoes are done, some of the skins may begin to split.

DRAIN the potatoes and run them under cold water.

PUT the potatoes in a bowl.

REFRIGERATE them overnight. *This step is the key to this cooking method.*

NEXT day, cut smaller potatoes into 4 pieces, larger ones into 6 or 8 pieces.

PLACE them in a large bowl, and add the remaining ingredients.

STIR to fully blend ingredients.

TASTE to adjust seasonings.

REFRIGERATE until ready to serve.

Tip: Wholesale shopping clubs sell the ranch dressing mix in a canister.

Note: If serving the next day, refrigerate as is, and add mayonnaise to taste just before serving as the potatoes will absorb the mayonnaise.

Do-Ahead Tip: This potato salad can be made two days in advance. The potatoes can be cooked four days in advance and refrigerated.

Country Baked Beans

Serves 10

1 32-ounce can **baked beans**
1/8 cup dried minced **onions**
1/2 cup **brown sugar**
3/4 cup **ketchup**
1 teaspoon yellow **prepared mustard**
1/3 cup **maple syrup**
2 chopped **chipotle chilies** with the juices which
    accumulate while chopping them
1 pound cured **kielbasa**, split lengthwise and cut into
    1/3" thick slices

PREHEAT the oven to 350 degrees.

STIR all the ingredients together in a big bowl.

POUR into a 15"x10" baking dish.

BAKE one hour until bubbling around the edges.

Do-Ahead Tip: *The beans can be prepared three days in advance. Cover and refrigerate until ready to bake.*

"Not Flat"
Chocolate Chip Cookies

Makes 24 3" cookies

1 cup **butter**, use cold butter and warm each stick only 8
    seconds in the microwave
3/4 cup packed **brown sugar**
1/2 cup granulated **sugar**
2 teaspoons **vanilla**
1 **egg**
2 1/2 cups **flour**
1/2 teaspoon **salt**
1 teaspoon **baking soda**
12 ounces **semi-sweet chocolate chips**

PREHEAT the oven to 375 degrees.

CREAM the butter and sugars well with a hand mixer.

ADD the vanilla and egg, mixing well.

ADD the flour, salt, and baking soda, blending until fine crumbs
form.

ADD the chocolate chips and stir into mixture until a uniform
dough results.

USING a 1 3/4" ice cream scoop, place scoops of dough on
ungreased cookie sheets, spacing twelve scoops per cookie sheet.

BAKE 8-10 minutes, or until the cookies are golden brown and no
longer look 'wet' in the center.

  *Do-Ahead Tip: This dough can be made two weeks in advance,
formed into balls, and frozen. Do not thaw before baking.*

Scratch Lemonade

Serves 6

grated **zest of two lemons**
2 cups **sugar**
2 cups **water**
2 cups **fresh lemon juice** using 6-8 lemons
3 cups **water**

COMBINE zest, sugar and water in a saucepan.

BRING to a full boil, stirring to melt the sugar.

REMOVE from the heat and transfer to a pitcher to cool.

REFRIGERATE the sugar syrup.

MIX the lemon juice and water.

REFRIGERATE the lemon water.

FILL glasses with ice and pour the lemon water over the ice to about 3/4 full.

ALLOW each person to add the sugar syrup to their own taste.

OR combine all the syrup and lemon water in one pitcher, and pour over ice in the glasses.

Do-Ahead Tip: *The lemon water and syrup can be prepared three days in advance.*

Scratch Lemonade

"He didn't tell me how to live;
he lived,
and let me watch him do it."

~ Clarence Budington Kelland

Father's Day Favorites

Potato Leek Soup

Rosemary Flank Steak

Twice Baked Potatoes

Smashed Cauliflower

Slow Cooker Coconut Rice Pudding

Coconut Cream Pie

Bourbon Slush

Let's start with dessert first! It sounds trite to say that the way to a man's heart is through his stomach, but I believe it. Quite a few men have proposed marriage to me when they tasted my homemade pies. One host even grabbed the rest of a Coconut Cream Pie from my hands after he took a bite, and then hid it in the refrigerator from the rest of the guests. This **Coconut Cream Pie** was adapted from a recipe that my friend Nancy got from her mother-in-law. So many of our favorite recipes are the ones we get from someone else.

If you are too busy to make the Coconut Cream Pie, make the **Slow Cooker Coconut Rice Pudding** instead. It is adapted from Lora Brody's recipe in her book Slow Cooker Cooking. If you think slow cooker gourmet is an oxymoron, you haven't tried Lora's recipes! The coconut flavor is muted in the finished pudding, and it couldn't be easier!

The **Potato Leek Soup** recipe, and a few others in this book, came from my friend Mary Sue who is a great cook. She made it using a pressure cooker, but I've always been afraid of them. This soup is rich and satisfying and has the added bonus of being low-fat. You can add a touch of heavy cream at the end, but even without it, people will think it's a cream soup. You absolutely must have a stick blender for this soup, as I refuse to recommend to anyone that they use a food processor to puree soup in batches. It makes a horrible mess and leaves you cranky.

Over thirty years ago **Rosemary Flank Steak** was the first dish I ever served at a dinner party. I was rather poor and flank steak was cheap because most people didn't know what to do with it. The recipe was forgotten for twenty years until I ran across it while working on this cookbook. I still love this dish and I think you will, too. You can also finish this recipe in a slow cooker. At the point where you add the wine and other ingredients, transfer everything to a slow cooker. Cook on low for six hours or on high for two hours.

The Rosemary Flank Steak is great on buttered egg noodles, but for those men who must have potatoes with their meat, I have included the recipe for **Twice Baked Potatoes**, a favorite comfort food. When I serve them at catered events, I figure two per person, as people always come back for seconds. Play with the recipe - add your favorite kind of cheese, bacon, sautéed vegetables, roasted garlic, or even those canned fried onions, if you like them!

I developed the recipe for the **Smashed Cauliflower** during the Atkins' Diet craze. It is low carb, but more importantly, it's really delicious. Cauliflower has never been a vegetable to get anyone excited, but you will want to make this recipe often. Cauliflower now comes in many colors such as purple and orange, if you want some extra color on the plate.

There are different versions of the **Bourbon Slush** drink in many cookbooks. I tinkered with this one until it was just the right thing to have on a hot afternoon. However, beware - they are quite addictive!

This whole meal can be made days ahead of time, leaving you time to enjoy the visit with your Dad.

Potato Leek Soup

Serves 6

4 tablespoons **butter**
3 cups sliced **leeks**, white parts only
1 unpeeled **carrot**, cut in big chunks
3 stalks sliced **celery**
1/2 medium **zucchini**, cut in chunks
4 sliced **potatoes** (peel if they are russets)
6 cups **chicken broth**
1/4 teaspoon each **salt** and **pepper**
1/4 cup **heavy cream**, optional

SAUTE leeks (supplement with onions if necessary), celery, carrot and zucchini in a soup pot with the butter, until the leeks are translucent.

ADD the potatoes and chicken broth.

SIMMER, covered, two hours or until all vegetables are soft and mushy.

PUREE with a stick blender, or in the food processor in batches.

SEASON with salt and pepper to taste.

Optional: For a richer soup, add the heavy cream.

Do-Ahead Tip: This soup can be made three days in advance or two weeks ahead and frozen.

Rosemary Flank Steak

Rosemary Flank Steak

Serves 4-6

2 pounds **flank steak**
1/4 cup, plus 2 tablespoons **butter**
2 cloves minced **garlic**
1/4 cup chopped fresh **parsley**
1/2 teaspoon **salt**
1 teaspoon dried or 1 tablespoon fresh **rosemary**
1/2 teaspoon dried **basil**
1/2 teaspoon dried **oregano**
8 ounces **tomato sauce**
1 cup **red wine**
12 ounces sliced fresh **mushrooms**
1 tablespoon **Wondra** quick-mixing flour
1 pound **egg noodles**
chopped **fresh parsley** for garnish, optional

SLICE the flank steak across the grain in 1/4" thick slices.

MELT 1/4 cup butter in a medium stock pot.

SAUTE the flank steak until browned on all sides.

ADD the garlic, parsley, salt, rosemary, basil, oregano, tomato sauce, and wine to the stock pot.

COVER and simmer over low heat for an hour.

ADD the mushrooms and cook ten minutes.

PREPARE the noodles according to package directions.

WHEN the noodles are done, drain them and return to the pan.

ADD 2 tablespoons butter to the noodles while hot and stir to melt.

ADD Wondra to the steak, a little at a time until the sauce is the desired thickness.

SERVE the steak immediately over hot, buttered noodles.

GARNISH with chopped parsley, if desired.

Optional: Beef broth can be substituted for the red wine.

Do-Ahead Tip: This recipe can be prepared two days in advance.

Twice Baked Potatoes

Serves 8

10 large **russet potatoes**
1/2 cup **butter**
1 cup **sour cream**
1 teaspoon **black pepper**
1 1/2 teaspoons **kosher salt**
1 teaspoon **garlic powder**
1/3 cup, plus 3 tablespoons **Parmesan cheese**
paprika

PREHEAT the oven to 375 degrees.

BAKE the potatoes until they test done, about an hour and a half.

REMOVE the potatoes from the oven.

LOWER the oven temperature to 350 degrees.

CUT the potatoes in half lengthwise.

SCOOP the insides of the potatoes into a bowl.

ADD 1/3 cup of the Parmesan cheese, and the remaining ingredients, **except** for the paprika.

USING a hand potato masher, mash the potatoes until there are no large lumps, then stir to incorporate all the ingredients.

SPOON the potato mixture back into only fifteen of the skins. Discard the extra five half skins or put aside to make baked potato skins at another time.

PLACE the stuffed potato skins on a heavy baking sheet and sprinkle with paprika and the 3 tablespoons of Parmesan cheese.

BAKE 30 minutes at 350 degrees.

SERVE immediately.

Note: The potatoes will hold in a 200 degree oven for an hour if necessary.

Do-Ahead Tip: The stuffed potatoes can be prepared three days in advance. When ready to serve bake 45 minutes at 350 degrees.

Smashed Cauliflower

Serves 6-8

1 medium head **cauliflower**
1 teaspoon, plus 1/2 teaspoon **salt**
6 tablespoons **butter**
3/4 cup **heavy cream**
1/8 teaspoon **garlic powder**
1/2 cup, plus 2 tablespoons **Parmesan cheese**
1/4 teaspoon **black pepper** or to taste
2 tablespoons **plain bread crumbs**

PREHEAT the oven to 400 degrees.

CLEAN, core and cut the cauliflower into florets.

PLACE the florets and 1 teaspoon salt in a sauce pan, cover with water and boil until tender.

DRAIN and return to the sauce pan.

MASH with a potato masher.

ADD 1/2 teaspoon salt, 1/2 cup Parmesan cheese, the butter, cream, garlic powder, and black pepper to the hot, mashed cauliflower.

MIX thoroughly.

TRANSFER the cauliflower mixture into a large, lightly greased pie plate or quiche dish, and level out.

TOP with the bread crumbs and 2 tablespoons Parmesan cheese.

BAKE 30 minutes, or until the Parmesan cheese starts to brown.

Note: During the baking process, the consistency becomes more like mashed potatoes.

Do-Ahead Tip: This recipe can be prepared two days in advance of baking.

Rosemary Flank Steak
Smashed Cauliflower

Slow Cooker Coconut Rice Pudding

Serves 6-8

1 cup uncooked **Arborio rice**
4 cups **half-and-half**
1 14-ounce can **cream of coconut** (not coconut milk)
dash **salt**
3 tablespoons **butter**
2 teaspoons **vanilla**
1/3 cup **raisins** or dried **cranberries**, if desired
cinnamon for dusting the top

PLACE the rice, half-and-half and the cream of coconut in a slow cooker.

STIR well.

COVER and cook on low for 2 hours.

ADD the salt, butter, vanilla and raisins or cranberries.

COOK uncovered another twenty minutes.

PLACE in a serving bowl and dust the top with cinnamon, if desired.

SERVE either warm or cold.

REFRIGERATE leftovers.

Do-Ahead Tip: *This pudding can be made three days in advance.*

Coconut Cream Pie

Serves 8-10

1/4 cup **coconut**
1 baked **pie shell**
4 **eggs**
1 cup **heavy cream**
1 1/3 cups **milk**
1 1/2 cups, plus 1/2 cup **flaked coconut**
1/2 cup **sugar**
1 teaspoon **vanilla**
1/4 teaspoon **coconut extract**
1/4 teaspoon **salt**
2 cups **heavy cream,** whipped until stiff with 1/3 cup
    confectioner's sugar

PREHEAT the oven to 350 degrees.

SCATTER 1/4 cup coconut on a cookie sheet.

BAKE 5-7 minutes until toasted to a golden brown. Watch carefully.

SET aside to cool.

BEAT the eggs, cream, milk, 1 1/2 cups coconut, sugar, vanilla, coconut extract and salt well with a hand mixer.

POUR the mixture into a buttered 9" glass pie plate.

PUT the pie plate in a flat-bottomed roasting pan and add hot water halfway up the side of the pie plate.

BAKE 40 minutes.

REMOVE from the oven, then remove pie plate from the roasting pan.

COOL at room temperature for several hours.

CAREFULLY slide the custard into the baked pie shell. If the custard seems to be sticking around the edges, gently loosen it with the edge of a knife or spatula.

TOP the custard with the additional 1/2 cup of flaked coconut and follow with whipped cream.

GARNISH with the toasted coconut.

REFRIGERATE until ready to serve.

Do-Ahead Tip: *This pie can be made a day in advance.*

Bourbon Slush

Makes 8 13-ounce servings

2 cups **water**
4 **tea bags**
2 cups **sugar**
7 cups of **water**
12 ounces thawed **frozen orange concentrate**
6 ounces thawed **frozen lemonade concentrate**
2 cups **bourbon**
lemon peel twist, optional

BOIL two cups of water.

ADD the teabags, and steep for four minutes.

REMOVE the teabags.

ADD the sugar.

STIR until the sugar is dissolved.

PUT seven cups of water, the tea/sugar mixture, orange juice concentrate, lemonade concentrate and bourbon into a large container for mixing.

PLACE in manageable freezer containers and freeze. Because of the alcohol and sugar, it will not freeze solid and will remain scoop-able.

WHEN ready to serve, fill iced tea glasses with scoops of slush and garnish with lemon peel twist if desired.

SERVE immediately with a straw or an iced tea spoon.

Do-Ahead Tip: *This recipe can be made a week in advance.*

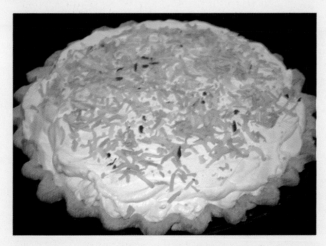

Coconut Cream Pie

64

"Nothing is more memorable
than a smell.
One scent can be
unexpected, momentary and fleeting,
yet conjure up a childhood summer
beside a lake in the mountains."

~ Diane Ackerman

Lake George Summer Luncheon

Panzanella Salad

Moroccan Lentil Salad

Shrimp Salad

Lobster Salad on Sliced Avocado

Flank Steak Blue Cheese Salad

Perfect Apricot Tart

White Sangria

Perhaps because our winters are so long, Adirondackers enjoy summer with a vengeance. From anywhere in the Adirondacks, it is a short trip to swim, fish, boat, camp, or hike. We joke that the lake water is only warm enough to swim in on the Fourth of July weekend but cold water never bothers the hundreds of Polar Bears, people of questionable sanity who plunge into Lake George every New Year's day! Another hardy bunch of souls are the 46'ers: people who have hiked each of 46 different local peaks and mountains. Being a "46'er" is quite the status symbol in this neck of the woods.

The season for entertaining outside is short. I love to serve this menu to good friends on my front porch. I've included three main dish salads for you to choose from. Everything is done ahead so that aside from quick dashes for the next course, I get to enjoy the party, too.

There are references to **Panzanella Salad** which date back to the 1500's in Italian literature. In the authentic recipes, completely stale bread is soaked in water, then wrung dry and tossed with garden fresh vegetables and a simple dressing of oil and vinegar. In this newer version, inspired by Ina Garten, cubes of fresh bread are oven toasted. If you are lucky enough to have heirloom tomatoes, this is the dish in which to use them.

Even though the **Lobster Salad on Sliced Avocado** must be prepared the morning of the day it will be served, it's worth it. For a more economical dish, you can substitute shrimp for half of the lobster. Check with a local food distributor who wholesales to restaurants and see if they will sell to you. Chances are you can save quite a bit of money this way. Figure about 4 ounces (1/2 cup) of lobster salad for each person, and half an avocado each. There may not be anything quite as luscious as lobster and avocado on the same plate.

The cooking method for the shrimp in the **Shrimp Salad** is also great to use for preparing cocktail shrimp. The **Flank Steak Blue Cheese Salad** is simple, but really satisfying. Serve it with dark beer and some small bakery rolls.

What's in a name? Actually, a lot. The first time I served the **Moroccan Lentil Salad**, I called it a curried lentil salad and it sat untouched. The next time around, I labeled it Moroccan Lentil Salad and a star was born. It has a wonderful chewiness, and because you are using freshly combined spices instead of a bottled curry powder, it has a fresh, interesting flavor. Your vegetarian friends will demand the recipe. You can find the red lentils at an ethnic market. They are actually bright orange when raw and yellow when cooked, so go figure!

When you find apricots that are more red than orange at the market, make the **Perfect Apricot Tart**. That advice will make this tart a once-a-year treat. But what better than an exquisite fruit tart to mark the passing of another year, like a Halloween pumpkin or the first snowfall? I start checking for ripe apricots right after my stargazer lilies are done blooming, moving happily from one gift of nature to another.

If you don't have a large crystal pitcher, buy one so your guests will see the beautiful variety of fruits floating in the **White Sangria**. I like to serve this drink with cocktail forks so that the fruit can be enjoyed when the wine is gone.

Panzanella Salad

Serves 8

Bread

small loaf of **French bread**, or one mini boule
3 tablespoons **olive oil**
kosher or sea **salt**

PREHEAT the oven to 400 degrees.

CUT the bread into 1" cubes, without removing the crust.

PLACE the bread cubes in a bowl.

ADD the salt and olive oil, and toss until thoroughly coated.

SPREAD the bread cubes in a single layer on a heavy baking sheet.

BAKE 10-15 minutes or until medium golden brown.

COOL completely, especially if planning to bag the bread cubes for future use.

Do-Ahead Tip: *The bread can be prepared one week in advance. Do not refrigerate.*

Dressing

2 small cloves minced **garlic**
1/2 teaspoon **Dijon mustard**
3 tablespoons **white balsamic vinegar**
1/2 cup **olive oil**
1/2 teaspoon kosher or sea **salt**
1/4 teaspoon freshly ground **black pepper**

WHISK all the ingredients vigorously until well combined.

SET aside.

Do-Ahead Tip: *The dressing can be prepared three days in advance.*

Vegetables

2 large **tomatoes,** cut into 1" cubes
1 **European cucumber**, halved lengthwise, seeds
    removed, cut into 1/2" slices
1 **red bell pepper**, cut into 1" cubes
1 **yellow** or **orange bell pepper**, cut into 1" cubes
1/2 thinly sliced **red onion**
5 large or 10 small **basil leaves**, thinly sliced
1/4 cup **capers**, drained
1/3 cup pitted **Kalamata olives**, optional

TOSS together the bread and vegetables when ready to serve.

ADD the dressing and toss until all ingredients are well coated.

Do-Ahead Tip: *The vegetables can be cut up a day in advance and stored in individual 'zip' bags in the refrigerator.*

Moroccan Lentil Salad

Serves 12

3 cups dried **red lentils**
1 1/2 cups finely chopped **red onions**
1 cup dried **currants**
1 fresh chopped **mango**, optional
1 cup chopped **fresh parsley**
1/3 cup drained **capers**
1 cup frozen **baby peas**, thawed
1/2 cup **red wine vinegar**
1/4 cup **Dijon mustard**
1 tablespoon **turmeric**
1 teaspoon kosher **salt**
1 teaspoon ground **cumin**
1/2 teaspoon ground **black pepper**
1/2 teaspoon ground **coriander**
1/2 teaspoon ground **mace**
1/4 teaspoon ground **cardamom**
1/4 teaspoon ground **cloves**
1/4 teaspoon ground **nutmeg**
1/4 teaspoon ground **cinnamon**
1/4 teaspoon **cayenne pepper**
1 1/2 cups vegetable or **canola oil**

BOIL 3 quarts of water in a large stock pot and add the lentils.

COOK for exactly two minutes.

TURN off the burner, and let stand for exactly five minutes.

DRAIN immediately, making sure the holes in the colander are smaller than the lentils, and run cold water over the lentils until completely cooled.

PUT the red onions, currants, mango, parsley, capers, peas and lentils in a large bowl.

PREPARE the dressing by placing the wine vinegar, mustard, turmeric, salt, black pepper, cumin, coriander, mace, cardamom, cloves, nutmeg, cayenne pepper, and cinnamon in a blender or food processor and blend until thoroughly mixed.

WHILE continuing to blend, add the oil and pulse until smooth.

POUR the dressing over the lentil mixture, and stir well.

Note: Red lentils are more easily found in an Indian or Oriental food supply store.

Do-Ahead Tip: This salad can be made three days in advance.

Shrimp Salad

Serves 8

Shrimp

3 tablespoons kosher **salt** or sea salt
1 **lemon**, cut into six pieces
4 pounds **raw shrimp**, 16-20 count size

PEEL and de-vein the shrimp, dividing into two equal portions.
BRING 5 quarts of water, the lemon and the salt to a full boil.
ADD half the shrimp to the boiling mixture.
TURN the heat down to medium high, and cook exactly three minutes.
REMOVE the shrimp with a slotted spoon into a colander and rinse with cold water.
RETURN the water to a boil and repeat with the remaining shrimp.
CUT each cooked shrimp into three pieces.
COOL completeiy.

Dressing

2 cups Hellmann's **mayonnaise**
1 teaspoon **Dijon mustard**
2 tablespoons **white balsamic vinegar**
1 teaspoon freshly ground **black pepper**
6 tablespoons minced **fresh dill** (do not use dry dill)

WHISK vigorously to combine all the ingredients.

Assembly

3 cups thinly sliced **celery**

COMBINE the shrimp and the celery with one third of the dressing.
TOSS, adding more dressing to taste.

Note: Do not mix this salad before the day to be served as the vinegar may toughen the shrimp.

Do-Ahead Tip: The shrimp can be poached two days in advance and the dressing can be made a week ahead. The salad can be assembled the morning of serving it.

Lobster Salad on Sliced Avocado

Lobster Salad
on
Sliced Avocado

Serves 6-8

2 pounds frozen pre-cooked **lobster meat**
3/4 cup Hellmann's **mayonnaise**
3/4 cup **sour cream**
1 cup chopped **celery**
4 tablespoons **ketchup**
1/3 cup prepared **horseradish** or to taste
1/4 teaspoon **onion salt**
1/2 teaspoon **black pepper**
3 perfectly ripe Haas **avocadoes**

THAW and drain the lobster. Break larger pieces into bite size chunks, disposing of any shell fragments and cartilage.

PLACE the lobster in a bowl and add the remaining ingredients, **except** the avocado.

ADD more mayonnaise and sour cream to moisten to taste.

TASTE to adjust seasonings.

WHEN ready to serve, cut each avocado in half, peel and cut each half into 6 slices, fanning them out on individual serving plates.

TOP with 1/2 cup of the lobster salad and serve immediately.

Do-Ahead Tip: *The lobster salad can be made earlier in the day.*

Perfect Apricot Tart

Flank Steak Blue Cheese Salad

Serves 6

Flank Steak

2 pound **flank steak**
1/2 cup **vegetable oil**
1/4 cup low sodium **soy sauce**
2 minced cloves **garlic**
3 tablespoons **balsamic vinegar**
2 tablespoons **mirin**
1 quarter sized piece **ginger**, minced
2 chopped **scallions**

COMBINE all ingredients except steak in a 'zip' bag, mixing well.

INSERT the flank steak into the bag and let the meat marinate overnight in the refrigerator.

REMOVE the flank steak when ready to grill.

GRILL the flank steak to medium rare, discarding the remaining marinade.

ALLOW the steak to cool at room temperature to avoid excess juices when mixing the salad.

Dressing

1 cup **sour cream**
3/4 cup Hellmann's **mayonnaise**
8 ounces crumbled **blue cheese**
dash **Worcestershire sauce**
1-2 tablespoons **milk**

COMBINE all the ingredients, blending well, adding enough milk to obtain the consistency preferred.

Salad

1 bag of three **romaine hearts**, chopped
6 sliced **plum tomatoes**
1 small **red onion**, thinly sliced
6 button **mushrooms**, sliced
5 sliced **radishes**
blue cheese crumbles, optional

DIVIDE the chopped romaine onto 6 salad or small dinner plates.

TOP with remaining salad ingredients.

SLICE the flank steak as thinly as possible and divide it evenly among the plates.

SPRINKLE with some additional blue cheese crumbles, if desired.

PASS the dressing separately.

Note: *The steak must be marinated the night before grilling.*

Do-Ahead Tip: *The dressing can be made three days in advance, and actually improves in flavor during that time. The salad vegetables can be prepared the day before, storing each separately in 'zip' bags.*

Perfect Apricot Tart

Serves 8-10

1 1/2 cups **flour**
6 tablespoons, plus 1 cup **confectioner's sugar**
3/4 cup **butter**, cut into pieces
2 teaspoons **vanilla**
18 perfectly **ripe apricots**, unpeeled and halved, pits
     removed
1/3 cup **apricot jam**, melted in a saucepan

PREHEAT the oven to 350 degrees.

TO make the crust, put the flour and six tablespoons of the confectioner's sugar into a food processor and pulse to combine.

ADD the butter and vanilla and process on high until a ball of dough forms.

WRAP the dough in plastic wrap.

FLATTEN and put into the refrigerator for at least an hour.

ROLL the dough out onto a silicone mat or between two sheets of plastic wrap, into a circle a few inches larger than the 12" round tart pan.

PICK up the mat (or plastic wrap with top layer removed) and invert, carefully dropping the crust into the pan.

SMOOTH out, being careful not to stretch the dough. Trim any crust overhang and discard.

SPRINKLE 1/2 cup of the confectioner's sugar evenly onto the crust.

TOP with apricots, cut side down, placed side by side in concentric circles working from the outside into the center.

SPRINKLE the remaining 1/2 cup of the confectioner's sugar over the top of the apricots.

BAKE 40-45 minutes until the crust is a dark golden brown. Most of the confectioner's sugar will have dissolved.

WHILE the tart is still hot, brush the tops of the apricots with the melted jam, just to coat.

Do-Ahead Tip: *The dough can be made two days in advance and refrigerated until ready to use. This tart is best made the morning it will be served.*

White Sangria

Serves 12

2 750 ml bottles **white wine**, preferably a Spanish
    vin rioja
2 cups **peach schnapps**, add more for a sweeter
    result
2 white **nectarines**, unpeeled and sliced
2 navel **oranges**, rind sliced off and cut into 1" sections
3 fresh **apricots**, unpeeled and sliced
3 white **peaches**, unpeeled and sliced

WASH the fruit, and prepare as directed.

COMBINE all the ingredients in a large glass pitcher and put in
the refrigerator until ready to serve.

Optional: *If served with cocktail forks, the guests can enjoy the
fruit in their glasses when the sangria is gone.*

Do-Ahead Tip: *This recipe must be prepared the day before
serving to allow the ingredients time to marinate.*

Adirondack
Hot Air Balloon
Festival Party

Gert's Corn Chowder

Pesto Pork Roast

Low-Fat Butternut Squash

Grandma Dott's Red Cabbage

Gail's Excellent Apple Crisp

Aunt Sally's Famous Carrot Cake

Mulled Cider

If you've never been to the Adirondacks, and can't get here in the summer, then come during the weekend of the Adirondack Hot Air Balloon Festival, which takes place at the Warren County Airport. Get up early enough for the 6 a.m. launch and you'll understand why this event is so near and dear to the hearts of Adirondackers. As you park on the airport runway and start walking through the morning mist toward the one hundred-plus balloons, you hear the hissing of the propane burners and suddenly, you are surrounded by bloating behemoths in many shapes and sizes. My favorite is the Flying Purple People Eater.

Walter and Joan Grishkot are the founders of the festival and have kept it running successfully for over 35 years. This festival is one of the very few which allows spectators to walk right up to the balloons as they inflate. There are five launches over four days, and the specialty balloons are not to be missed.

Ever since my daughter Sara was five months old, she and I have chased hot air balloons during the festival. We look up and pick one, then set out on a wild chase to wherever the balloon may land. If we're lucky, the crew invites us to help fold up the balloon, and sometimes they will offer us a short tethered ride. It's traditional for the balloon pilot to give a bottle of champagne to the owner of the property he lands on. Even if you don't go to the airport for any of the launches, you are bound to glimpse dozens of floating balloons as you drive around town. It is something everyone must see at least once, and something you will never forget!

Gathering for the evening launch is a favorite thing to do for those of us living close enough to the airport to see it from a distance. It's magical to sit on a patio on a brisk fall day, while sipping hot mulled cider and watching dozens of hot air balloons pass overhead. The perfect excuse for a dinner party! Every dish in this meal can be prepared days ahead, except for roasting the pork.

Gert's Corn Chowder is decidedly not low fat, with its bacon drippings and half & half, but people love it. "Gert" is Virginia O'Brien, the mother of my childhood friend, Mary Jo. For this menu, serve small cups of the soup leaving your guests eager for the rest of the meal. Make this soup when you have about two cups of roasted potatoes left over from a dinner, which will reduce the cooking time for the soup to half an hour.

The **Pesto Pork Roast** is, in the words of a friend, "outrageous" in a good way! It can be stuffed and rolled the evening before the dinner and popped into the oven when your guests arrive. The roasting juices of the parsley pesto and the pork combine to make a terrific pan gravy. I've included directions for extending the pan gravy by adding a package of pork gravy mix, because we never seem to have enough gravy, but you can leave it out for even better flavor.

I love the color of the **Low-Fat Butternut Squash** on the plate next to the pork roast. You'll never believe there is no butter in the squash. It's that delicious. My **Grandma Dott's Red Cabbage** adds even more color contrast, and it's hearty and satisfying.

My grandmother's family in Poland was so poor, they subsisted largely on potatoes. When my grandmother got here at the age of fourteen, she vowed to never eat another potato. She lived to be eighty-six and to my knowledge, she kept that promise. So, in honor of the memory of Matilda Dott, I left potatoes out of this menu. And it makes a great story for the dinner.

My sister Gail makes **Gail's Excellent Apple Crisp** for her kids, sometimes more than once in the same weekend during apple-picking season here in the Adirondacks. It tastes best using crisp McIntosh apples straight from the orchard. The crumb topping is the best I have had and can also be used to top muffins.

Aunt Sally's Famous Carrot Cake reminds you why you ever liked carrot cake in the first place. It is moist and simple - no coconut or raisins lurking here. I don't peel the carrots before I grate them making preparation a little faster. The cream cheese frosting purposely has no vanilla in it, so the delicate cream cheese flavor stands out.

If at all possible, when making the **Mulled Cider**, go to an apple orchard to buy the cider. I have an inexpensive 30 cup electric coffee pot which I use exclusively for mulled cider. This gets the cider circulating through the spices and keeps it hot until ready to drink.

There are many "you-pick" apple orchards in the Adirondacks. Some allow you to drive right into the orchard, and others load you onto rickety wooden carts pulled by wheezing tractors. Most all of them sell freshly made cider doughnuts, pumpkins of all sizes, and warty decorative gourds. We wait for a sunny day to go to the orchard on our annual outing. As we bounce along in the cart, we turn our faces toward the weakening sun to soak up the dregs of summer, and we give ourselves over to a new season.

I do believe fall is my favorite time of year.

Gert's Corn Chowder

Serves 8

1 pound **bacon**
1 large **onion**, diced
2 16-ounce cans **creamed corn**
2 cups **half-and-half**
2 cups **milk**
3 large or four medium **potatoes**, unpeeled and cut
    into 1/2" dice
1 tablespoon **fresh corn kernels**
1/2 teaspoon **black pepper**

FRY the bacon in a stockpot until crispy.

REMOVE to drain on paper towels.

SET aside one slice of the bacon to use for garnishing.

ONCE the bacon is cool enough to handle, crumble.

DISCARD about 1/4 of the remaining bacon grease.

SAUTE the diced onion in the remaining bacon grease until translucent.

ADD the remaining ingredients, including the crumbled bacon and simmer on medium low for an hour, stirring occasionally.

TEST the potatoes for tenderness. If not tender, continue simmering the potatoes are done.

GARNISH individual servings with a bit of the reserved bacon strip, crumbled, and a few fresh corn kernels.

Optional: Two cups of leftover cooked, diced potatoes can be substituted for the raw potatoes. By doing so, this soup can be ready to eat in half an hour!

Do-Ahead Tip: This chowder can be made three days in advance, and it freezes well. When thawed, it may need to be thinned with some milk or half-and-half.

Pesto Pork Roast

Serves 8

3 - 4 pound **center cut pork boneless loin roast**
Wondra quick-mixing flour
1 package **pork gravy mix**, mix as directed
1/2 teaspoon **black pepper**
1/2 teaspoon **garlic powder**

PREHEAT the oven to 325 degrees.

BUTTERFLY the roast, like a tri-fold brochure.

SPREAD the Parsley Pesto (recipe follows) over the entire surface.

ROLL up the roast, jelly roll style, and secure with toothpicks.

SPRINKLE the roast with black pepper and garlic powder.

PUT the prepared roast in a 15"x10" baking dish and cover tightly with foil, crimping the edges over the sides of the pan.

BAKE one hour until the interior temperature reaches 160 degrees.

REMOVE the pork roast to a slicing board to rest.

STRAIN the pan juices, if desired, and pour into a saucepan.

HEAT the juices to boiling, adding the pork gravy mix and water.

WHISK in just enough Wondra to thicken the gravy to taste.

REMOVE the toothpicks.

SLICE the roast.

SERVE immediately with the gravy on the side.

Do-Ahead Tip: *Prepare the roast the night before baking.*

Parsley Pesto

1 1/2 cups packed **flat leaf parsley**
1/2 cup packed leaves of **fresh basil**
1 1/4 cups **Parmesan cheese**
1/2 cup **pine nuts**
12 tablespoons **butter**
1/4 cup **olive oil**
1/2 teaspoon **salt**
1/4 teaspoon **black pepper**

PUT all the ingredients into a food processor and blend until uniform.

REFRIGERATE until an hour before proceeding with the recipe if not using the pesto right away.

Do-Ahead Tip: *This pesto can be made a week in advance.*

Low-Fat Butternut Squash

Serves 6-8

1 large or two small **butternut squash**
1 40-ounce can **chicken broth**
salt and **pepper** to taste

PEEL the squash and remove the seeds. Cut into chunks.

COMBINE the squash and chicken broth in a small stockpot.

BRING to a boil. Cover and continue boiling until the squash is very tender, usually an hour and a half.

DRAIN well and return the squash to the stockpot.

MASH with a potato masher.

ADD salt and pepper to taste, stirring well.

TRANSFER the squash to an oven safe two quart baking dish.

MICROWAVE, covered with plastic wrap, for 5-10 minutes or until heated throughout.

Do-Ahead Tip: *This squash can be made three days in advance.*

Pesto Pork Roast and Low-Fat Butternut Squash

Grandma Dott's Red Cabbage

Serves 10

6 slices raw **bacon**, diced
1 large **onion**, chopped
1 thinly sliced medium head of **red cabbage**
3 quartered and cored **apples**, any kind
4 tablespoons **cider vinegar** OR white balsamic
    vinegar
4 tablespoons **light brown sugar**
1 teaspoon **salt**
1/4 teaspoon **black pepper**, or to taste

IN an 8 quart stew pot, fry the diced bacon with the chopped onion until browned.

SLICE the apples 1/2" thick.

ADD the apples and the remaining ingredients to the stew pot.

SIMMER, uncovered, over medium low heat for three hours.

TOSS occasionally until the cabbage has wilted and is reduced to about one half its original volume.

Do-Ahead Tip: *This cabbage can be made three days in advance.*

Gail with her Apple Crisp

Aunt Sally's Famous Carrot Cake

Serves 10-12

2 cups, plus 1 tablespoon **flour**
2 cups **sugar**
1 teaspoon **salt**
1 teaspoon **baking soda**
2 teaspoons **cinnamon**
2 teaspoons **baking powder**
1 1/4 cups **vegetable oil**
4 **eggs**
2 teaspoons **vanilla**
2 cups unpeeled, grated **carrots**
20-ounce can crushed **pineapple**,
    drained and squeezed dry
1 cup broken **pecans**

PREHEAT the oven to 325 degrees.

BEAT the flour, sugar, salt, baking soda, cinnamon, baking power and vegetable oil with a hand mixer for two minutes.

ADD the eggs and vanilla.

BEAT two minutes longer.

ADD the carrots, pineapple and pecans.

STIR until well combined.

GREASE and flour two round 9" pans, three round 8" pans, or one 15"x10" baking dish. This recipe will make about eight dozen mini cupcakes, or about three and a half dozen regular sized cupcakes.

FILL the pans or cupcake papers no more than half full.

BAKE the cakes 40 minutes. Cupcakes take approximately 15 minutes for either size.

TEST for doneness with a toothpick. The cake is done when the tooth pick comes out dry.

COOL.

TURN one layer upside down on a serving plate.

SPREAD with a layer of Cream Cheese Frosting (recipe follows).

PLACE the remaining layer right side up on the frosted layer.

FROST with Cream Cheese Frosting.

Cream Cheese Frosting

16 ounces **cream cheese**
8 cups **confectioner's sugar**
chopped pecans, optional
small frosting carrots, optional

COMBINE the cream cheese and sugar in a bowl.
BEAT until it is a spreadable consistency.
FROST the cake or cupcakes.
GARNISH with the chopped pecans or small frosting carrots, if desired.

Do-Ahead Tip: *This cake can be made three days in advance and refrigerated.*

Gail's Excellent Apple Crisp

Serves 8-10

12 large **fresh McIntosh apples**
1/2 cup **water**
1/8 teaspoon **salt**
2 teaspoons **cinnamon**
1 1/2 cups **flour**
2 cups **sugar**
2/3 cup **butter**

PREHEAT the oven to 350 degrees.
GREASE AND FLOUR a 13"x9" pan.
PEEL, core and slice the apples.
PUT the sliced apples in a bowl with the water, salt and cinnamon.
TOSS to combine, and then spread this mixture evenly in the pan.
COMBINE the flour, sugar and butter with a pastry blender until obtaining uniformly sized crumbs.
SCATTER the crumb topping evenly over the top of the apple mixture.
BAKE 40-45 minutes.

Do-Ahead Tip: *This apple crisp can be made a day in advance.*

Pesto Pork Roast
Low-Fat Butternut Squash
Grandma Dott's Red Cabbage

Mulled Cider

Serves 20

1 gallon unfiltered **apple cider**
3 **cinnamon sticks**, broken in half
1 teaspoon **cinnamon**
3 **cardamom pods**
1 **star anise**
4 **whole cloves**
1 **vanilla bean**, split lengthwise
1 **apple**, unpeeled, thinly sliced
1 **orange**, unpeeled, thinly sliced
1/4 cup **sugar**, optional

COMBINE all the ingredients in a sauce pan.

SIMMER without boiling for half an hour.

STRAIN into a serving pitcher.

TRANSFER to a thermal carafe or pump pot to keep hot while serving.

Do-Ahead Tip: The cider can be made two days in advance with the exception of adding the apples and oranges. Strain and refrigerate. When ready to reheat, add the apples and oranges.

Gail's Excellent Apple Crisp

"...in the '50's
everybody went to a psychiatrist
because if you didn't,
you'd have nothing to talk about
at cocktail parties."

~ Rod Steiger

Do-Ahead Cocktail Party

Pork and Ginger Dumplings

Baked Brie with Granny Smith Apples

Asparagus Blue Cheese Rolls

Aunt Sally's Famous
Mushroom Knapsacks

Spinach Feta Filo Triangles

Green Eggs and Ham

Bacon Wrapped Scallops

Mini Filet Mignon Sandwiches

Judy Madison's Dinner Rolls

Lora Brody's Duck Paté

Mini Reubens

Chicken Captiva

If it must be said that Aunt Sally's Catering has a specialty, it would be my hors d'oeuvres. I love making ambrosial small bites. A tasty new entree always inspires me to wonder, "hmmm, can this be adapted to hors d'oeuvres size?"

Every one of these recipes is made completely ahead of time, some needing only a quick trip into the oven just before they are served. Some are ridiculously simple to prepare, and some of them can be frozen before baking, so why not? Then you'll always have goodies on hand for unexpected visitors who will wonder how you did it.

Aunt Sally's Famous Mushroom Knapsacks are my most popular hors d'oeuvre. I never thought I would part with this recipe. When people taste these, they recognize them as someone's labor of love. Guests have tried to take whole trays of them away from the server. We eventually had to develop a passing strategy for the mushroom knapsacks to ensure that everyone would get some! I sent the server outside and back in a different door so that the guests hovering outside the kitchen would not eat them all up. Bake the knapsacks until the tips and bottoms are medium golden brown. That is the flavor key to anything made with filo. Don't be afraid of filo if you have not used it before. My daughter, Sara, has been using it since she was eight years old.

You can make the filling for the **Spinach Feta Filo Triangles** days ahead of assembling them and then freeze the triangles for later use. They should go straight from the freezer to a preheated oven or they will look shriveled.

After many years of wrapping brie in puff pastry or filo dough and experimenting with peeling the brie, splitting the brie, or filling the brie, **Baked Brie with Granny Smith Apples** is the recipe I use now. It gets rave reviews and better yet: it must be prepared the night before you bake it.

I first served the **Green Eggs and Ham** for a client who wanted deviled eggs at her wedding, and she wanted them fiery! Deviled eggs may be seen as lowbrow fare, but every time I serve them, there is never a single one left. I added wasabi and garnished the piped eggs with tiny heart cutouts of smoked ham. The guests were so delighted, and the eggs were such a conversation piece, that I now serve them often.

Pork and Ginger Dumplings is a recipe which came from a guy I worked with briefly years ago, and all I remember is that his name was Thom, with an h. Thom's dumplings are to die for. I tweaked the recipe a bit by adding freshly grated ginger to the filling.

When you really have no spare time at all, the **Bacon Wrapped Scallops** and the **Mini Reubens** are just the things to prepare.

A recipe for the **Asparagus Blue Cheese Rolls** is found in many community cookbooks, including Junior League cookbooks, which are always good ones to have. You'll have fun being mysterious when you are asked what the dough is! The key to the great flavor is to make sure the rolls are golden brown on the edges and the bottoms. People often say, "I don't like asparagus or blue cheese, but I love these!" I don't think a better compliment exists.

Chicken Captiva started out as an entrée I had at a restaurant in Florida. Don't miss sampling the garlicky, browned cheese that sticks to the baking sheet - it's fantastic!

When I make the **Mini Filet Mignon Sandwiches**, I call Mary Ellen over at Sokol's Market to make the little butter knot rolls for me. I've also included my friend Judy Madison's recipe for rolls using a bread machine just in case you can't get to Sokol's!

This adaptation of the recipe for **Lora Brody's Duck Pâté** couldn't be easier to do. Preparing the duck in a slow cooker guarantees moist and tender meat. Preparation of the pâté is quick and easy using a food processor, and it can be made five days ahead because topping the ramekin with melted butter creates an airtight seal.

If you're serving hors d'oeuvres before a dinner party, select one or two that you really love along with simple things like nicoise olives, nuts, tiny cornichon pickles, or the spiced pecans which can be made weeks ahead. In this situation, less is more and those special hors d'oeuvres can shine.

For a full blown cocktail party that falls during dinner hour, offer at least eight or nine selections. To ensure that you have a good time, hire someone to man the oven and you will actually be able to enjoy your own party! No one has a good time at a party if the hostess is running around in a lather. They came to see you!

Mini Filet Mignon Sandwiches
Aunt Sally's Famous Mushroom Knapsacks
Asparagus Blue Cheese Rolls
Chicken Captiva
Pork and Ginger Dumplings

Pork and Ginger Dumplings

Makes 30 Pieces

Dough

2 cups **flour**
2/3 cup **boiling water**
1/4 cup **cold water**

PUT the flour in a mixing bowl.
STIR in the boiling water.
STIR in the cold water until dough forms.
COVER and set aside to rest while making the filling.

Filling

1/2 pound **freshly ground pork**, NOT sausage
1 thinly sliced **scallion**
1 cup small dice **bok choy**
1 tablespoon **dry white wine**
1 tablespoon low sodium **soy sauce**
1 1/2 teaspoons **cornstarch**
1 teaspoon **salt**
1/4 teaspoon **sugar**
1 1/2 teaspoons **freshly grated ginger**

PLACE all the filling ingredients in a bowl and combine to mix well.
SET aside.

Assembly

DIVIDE the prepared dough in half and roll out both halves on a heavily floured surface to about 1/16 inch thickness. Check under the dough during this process and dust with more flour to prevent sticking to the surface.

CUT circles with a 2 1/2" round cutter. By cutting all the circles during this step, it will be possible to prepare the remainder of this recipe in an assembly line fashion, making it quicker and easier.

PUT a heaping teaspoon of the filling on one side of each circle towards the center folding line.

MOISTEN half of the outer edge of the circle with water using a pastry brush.

FOLD the unfilled half of the circle over the filling and seal it by lightly squeezing the edges together.

STAND the dumpling on its base, with the sealed side pointing up, using slight pressure to make a flat bottom.

GENTLY make the sealed edge fluted, as on a pie crust.

ONCE formed, transfer the dumplings to a cookie sheet covered with plastic wrap or parchment paper. Do not let them touch each other as they will stick together.

COVER the whole pan with plastic wrap and freeze the dumplings.

Cooking

vegetable oil
1 can **chicken broth**

WHEN ready to serve, warm one tablespoon vegetable oil in a sauté pan.

ADD the frozen dumplings and cook until the bottoms become lightly browned.

POUR 1/3 cup chicken broth over the dumplings in the sauté pan.

COVER with a tight lid and cook for eight minutes on low.

REPEAT until all the dumplings have been cooked.

SERVE with Ginger Soy Dipping Sauce.

Ginger Soy Dipping Sauce

1/2 cup **soy sauce**
1/4 cup **water**
1 1/2 teaspoons **freshly grated ginger**

COMBINE and heat the ingredients in a sauce pan.

SERVE warm with the dumplings.

Do-Ahead Tip: Make the dough the morning of assembly. The filling can be made the day before, or a month in advance if frozen. The dipping sauce can be made a week earlier, but must be refrigerated until ready to use. Also, the dumplings can be fully cooked, covered with plastic wrap and reheated up to two days later in the microwave. Raw dumplings can be frozen a month in advance.

Baked Brie
with
Granny Smith Apples

Serves 6-8

1 one-pound **wheel of brie**, unwrapped
1 **granny smith apple**
1 cup **brown sugar**
1 large or 2 small sliced **baguettes**

PEEL, core, and slice the apple into small pieces about half the size of a postage stamp and about 1/4 inch thick.

PLACE the wheel of brie in a baking dish or pie plate not much larger than the brie itself.

TOP with the apple pieces.

SPRINKLE the brown sugar over the top, covering the apples.

REFRIGERATE overnight.

PREHEAT the oven to 400 degrees.

BAKE twenty minutes or until the center of the brie is visibly puffy.

SPREAD the hot brie on sliced baguettes.

TOP with a piece or two of the apple, using a small spoon to transfer the apple onto the brie.

KEEPING the brie warm will allow it to be easily served.

Do-Ahead Tip: *MUST prepare the night before baking.*

Asparagus Blue Cheese Rolls

Makes about 100 pieces

1 loaf of **white sandwich bread**, with a flat top
8 ounces softened **cream cheese**
4 ounces crumbled **blue cheese**
1 **egg**
2 dozen **asparagus spears**
1 cup **butter**

TRIM the crusts from 24 slices of white bread and flatten as much as possible with a rolling pin. Once trimmed and flattened, cover the slices in plastic wrap until ready to use.

PREPARE the asparagus spears by snapping off the root ends.

COMBINE the cream cheese, blue cheese and egg with a hand mixer.

SPREAD two tablespoons of the blue cheese filling to the edges on each slice of the flattened bread.

PLACE an asparagus spear across the top edge of each slice of bread, leaving the tip end hanging off. Cut off the overhanging tip with a knife.

ROLL up the slice, starting with the asparagus edge.

MELT the butter in the microwave, in a small flat-bottomed glass dish.

DIP each roll into the melted butter, covering completely.

PLACE the rolls on a cookie sheet lined with parchment or plastic wrap. The rolls should not be touching each other.
Cover with plastic wrap and freeze.

WHEN ready to serve, preheat the oven to 400 degrees.

REMOVE the rolls from the freezer for about ten minutes. Trim each end, and cut each roll into four pieces.

RETURN to a parchment lined cookie sheet, cut side up, and bake 10-12 minutes, or until the edges and bottoms are golden brown.

Note: *If possible, make the filling ahead of time and freeze it. When thawed and stirred, any lumps of blue cheese magically disappear, and it spreads smoothly.*

Do-Ahead Tip: *These rolls can be made and frozen a month in advance. They must be frozen before slicing. The blue cheese filling can be frozen for three months.*

Aunt Sally's Famous Mushroom Knapsacks

Makes about 100 pieces

24 ounces fresh **mushrooms**, coarsely chopped
4 tablespoons, plus 1 cup **butter**
1 teaspoon dried **minced onion**
1 teaspoon garlic **salt**
1 teaspoon **lemon juice**
1 teaspoon **Worcestershire sauce**
2 16-ounce packages **filo dough**, thawed overnight in the
    refrigerator
2 16-ounce packages **cream cheese**

PLACE the mushrooms, 4 tablespoons butter, minced onion, salt, lemon juice and Worcestershire sauce in a sauté pan and cook over medium heat until all the liquid has evaporated.

SET the mushroom filling aside to cool. Refrigerate or freeze until ready to assemble.

MELT one cup butter in the microwave. Cool for ten minutes.

USING the melted butter and a pastry brush, first butter the work surface and then three sheets of filo, stacking one on top of the other once buttered.

CUT the layered sheets into eight squares.

PLACE a piece of cream cheese about the size of a pearl onion onto each square.

TOP with one teaspoon of the mushroom filling.

GATHER the four corners of the filo and bring them together lightly. The butter will hold the dough in place. Be careful not to squeeze or twist the filo as it will crumble when it is baked.

PREHEAT the oven to 400 degrees.

PLACE the 'knapsacks' on a parchment lined baking sheet.

BAKE at 400 degrees for 10-15 minutes, or until the bottoms and edges are golden brown.

COOL for a few minutes and serve immediately.

Do-Ahead Tip: *The knapsacks can be made a day in advance and refrigerated. They can also be made weeks ahead and frozen, then put directly from the freezer into a preheated oven.*

Spinach Feta Filo Triangles

Makes 60 triangles

1/3 cup **olive oil**
1 1/2 cups diced **onion**
20 ounces frozen chopped **spinach**, thawed
1 cup **feta cheese**, crumbled
1 1/2 cups **ricotta cheese**
1 tablespoon crumbled **dry mint**
1 tablespoon dried **dill weed**
dash **nutmeg**
1/2 teaspoon **salt**
1/2 teaspoon **black pepper**
2 16-ounce packages **filo dough**
1/2 cup **butter**, melted, cooled for ten minutes

HEAT the oil in a sauce pan over medium heat.

SAUTE the onions until tender and almost golden.

SQUEEZE the juices out of the spinach until as dry as possible.

STIR the spinach into the oil and onions. Cook 5 minutes longer.

REMOVE from the heat and set aside to cool.

COMBINE the cooled spinach mixture in a bowl with the feta cheese, ricotta cheese, mint, dill weed, nutmeg, salt and pepper, stirring well.

SET aside while preparing the filo dough.

PREHEAT the oven to 375 degrees.

USING the melted butter and a pastry brush, first butter the work surface and then two sheets of filo, stacking one on top of the other.

CUT the layered sheets the long way into 4 strips for larger triangles.

PLACE a heaping teaspoon of filling on the bottom of each strip.

FOLD up like a flag, zigzagging back and forth until the entire strip has been used.

PLACE the triangles on a baking sheet lined with parchment.

BAKE 20 minutes, or until the filo becomes golden brown on the bottom and the edges.

COOL 10 minutes, and serve.

Do-Ahead Tip: The triangles can be made and frozen, uncooked, a month in advance. Frozen triangles should go directly from the freezer to a preheated oven. Bake 30 minutes.

Green Eggs and Ham

Makes 56 stuffed eggs

28 **eggs**
3/4 cup Hellmann's **mayonnaise**
1/3 cup **horseradish**, squeezed dry
4 teaspoons **wasabi powder**
1 teaspoon **salt**
green paste food coloring, leaf green preferred
4 slices **ham**

COVER eggs with cold water in a large sauce pan.

BRING to a full boil. Turn off burner, cover, and let sit for 20 minutes.

RUN cold water over the hard boiled eggs to cool.

PEEL.

CUT the eggs in half lengthwise.

REMOVE the yolks to a small mixing bowl.

PUT the egg whites on the serving platter.

CRUMBLE the yolks with a pastry blender.

ADD the mayonnaise, horseradish, and salt. For a creamier consistency, add another 1/4 cup of mayonnaise.

MIX well with a hand mixer.

ADD the wasabi powder a teaspoon at a time, taste testing while mixing to control the level of heat.

BLEND in just enough food coloring paste to give the yolks a pleasant light green color.

MOUND a spoonful of yolks back into the egg whites, or use a piping bag with a large tip to "stuff" the egg whites.

USING a tiny heart-shaped cutter (or other shape) about 1" across, make 56 cutouts from the stacked ham slices.

PLACE a cutout on top of each stuffed egg.

WRAP well with plastic wrap.

REFRIGERATE until ready to serve.

Do-Ahead Tip: The stuffed eggs can be made one day in advance. Wrap and refrigerate.

Bacon Wrapped Scallops

Makes 20-30

1 pound sea **scallops**, size 20-30
Precooked or **un-cooked bacon**, slices equal to the
number of scallops being prepared

IF using uncooked bacon, fry the slices to a pre-crisp stage.

DRAIN the partially cooked bacon on paper towels.

CUT any large scallops in half.

WRAP each scallop in a piece of precooked bacon and spear
through the middle with a plain wooden toothpick.

BROIL until browned, approximately about 5 minutes.

CHECK to see if they need to be turned over and browned.

COOL for a minute or two on paper towels and then serve.

Do-Ahead Tip: *These can be wrapped in bacon one day in
advance and refrigerated until ready to broil.*

Green Eggs and Ham

Mini Filet Mignon Sandwiches

Makes 36

4 pound trimmed **tenderloin of beef**
black pepper
garlic powder
1/2 cup **sour cream**
1/2 cup Hellmann's **mayonnaise**
3 tablespoons prepared **horseradish**
dash of **Worcestershire sauce**
36 **rolls** (recipe follows) or use 36 2" soft bakery rolls

PREHEAT the oven to 325 degrees.

AT least four hours before planning to serve these sandwiches, place the tenderloin on a heavy baking sheet and sprinkle liberally with black pepper and garlic powder.

BAKE 20 minutes.

USING a quick tip thermometer, check every 8-10 minutes until the internal temperature reaches 130 degrees.

REMOVE the beef from the oven and allow to cool at room temperature.

MEANWHILE, combine sour cream, mayonnaise, horseradish and Worcestershire sauce in a small bowl, stirring to combine.

SLICE the rolls in half, keeping tops and bottoms together.

SLICE the tenderloin into medallions slightly smaller than the size of the roll, and about 1/3" thick.

PLACE the slices on a plate covered with paper towels to soak up excess juices.

TOP the bottom of each roll with a dab of the horseradish sauce and a slice of the beef.

REPLACE the top of the roll.

PLAN to serve within half an hour once prepared.

Do-Ahead Tip: The sauce can be made three days in advance. Roast the meat the morning the sandwiches will be assembled and served. The rolls can be sliced the day ahead and covered with plastic wrap.

Judy Madison's Dinner Rolls

Makes 36 rolls
Bread machine recipe

3/4 cup **milk**, slightly warmed in the microwave
6 tablespoons softened **butter,** plus 4 tablespoons melted
    butter
1 large, slightly beaten **egg**
3 cups **flour**
1/4 cup **sugar**
1 teaspoon **salt**
1 1/2 teaspoons **active dry yeast**

USING the bread machine manufacturer's recommendations, measure all ingredients, **except** the 4 tablespoons of melted butter, into the bread machine pan.

SELECT the "dough" setting.

WHEN the dough cycle is complete, remove the dough, divide into 36 equal parts and form into balls.

PREHEAT the oven to 325 degrees.

ROLL each ball into a 6" rope and tie in a knot.

DIP rope knots in the melted butter.

PLACE the rolls on a greased baking sheet or parchment paper.

COVER the rolls with a cloth and let rise for about 20 minutes in a warm place until almost doubled in size.

BRUSH the tops with melted butter.

BAKE 15 minutes. Do not let the rolls turn dark brown as that toughens them.

***Do-Ahead Tip:** The rolls can be made two days in advance or made earlier and frozen either before or after baking them.*

Mini Filet Mignon Sandwiches

Lora Brody's Duck Pâté

Makes one pound

4 pound cleaned **duck**, giblets removed
6 unpeeled **garlic cloves**
10 sprigs **fresh rosemary**
10 sprigs **fresh thyme**
2 large **carrots**, peeled and cut into 4 pieces
1 cup **chicken broth**
sea **salt**
freshly ground **black pepper**

Duck

RINSE the duck inside and out and pat dry.

PLACE the duck, breast side down, in a 4 quart slow cooker.

ADD the cloves, rosemary and thyme to the slow cooker.

SCATTER the carrots around the duck.

ADD the chicken broth.

SPRINKLE the duck with salt and pepper.

COVER and cook on high for 6-8 hours, turning the duck halfway through the cooking time.

WHEN the meat is very tender, turn off the slow cooker and allow the duck to cool, covered, for 15 minutes.

REMOVE the duck to a bowl.

WHEN it is cool enough to handle, remove the meat from the bones.

CHOP up the duck meat and set aside.

STRAIN the stock into a bowl and discard the carrots and herbs.

PLACE the bowl of stock into the refrigerator.

ONCE the fat has congealed, skim it off, discarding it or reserving it for other uses if desired.

RESERVE the remaining stock.

Pâté

2 cups chopped **duck meat**
1/2 cup softened **butter**, plus 4 tablespoons melted **butter**
2 teaspoons dried **herbes de provence**
1 tablespoon **cognac**

3 tablespoons reserved **duck broth**
1/2 teaspoon **salt**
1 teaspoon **black pepper**
sliced **baguettes** or **crackers**
cornichon pickles, optional

PUT the two cups of duck meat chunks into a food processor.

PULSE until the duck meat is coarsely ground.

ADD 1/2 cup softened butter and process until smooth.

ADD the herbes de Provence, cognac, reserved duck broth, salt and pepper to taste.

PROCESS until incorporated.

SCRAPE the mixture into a 3 cup ramekin and pour the four tablespoons melted butter over the top.

REFRIGERATE the pâté until ready to serve.

SERVE with sliced baguettes or crackers, and cornichon pickles, if desired.

Do-Ahead Tip:
The pâté can be made five days before serving.

110

Mini Reubens

Makes 40 pieces

1 loaf **cocktail rye bread,**
    or **cocktail pumpernickel bread**
1/2 cup **Russian dressing**
20 slices quality **corned beef**
16 ounces **sauerkraut**, fresh or canned
20 slices **Swiss cheese**

PREHEAT the oven to 400 degrees.

LAY out the cocktail rye on cookie sheets in a single layer.

TOP each slice with about a teaspoon of Russian dressing, spreading to all corners.

TOP with one half of a corned beef slice, folding to fit the bread.

TOP with about a tablespoon of sauerkraut which has been drained and squeezed dry.

TOP with a piece of Swiss cheese, trimmed to fit the bread.

BAKE 10-12 minutes until the outline of the sauerkraut can be seen through the melted cheese.

> ***Optional:*** *To make "Rachels", substitute turkey breast for the corned beef.*

> ***Do-Ahead Tip:*** *These can be assembled and refrigerated one day in advance of baking.*

111

Chicken Captiva

Makes about 60 pieces

1 cup **butter** at room temperature
6 minced **garlic cloves**
1/3 cup chopped **fresh parsley**, tightly packed
2 tablespoons **fresh lemon juice**
pinch **salt**
3 pounds boneless, skinless **chicken breasts**, trimmed
extra **butter**
60 size 30-40 **shrimp**, cooked, peeled, de-veined,
      de-tailed, and thawed, if frozen
1 1/2 pounds **mozzarella cheese**

PUT the butter, garlic, parsley, lemon juice and salt into a medium bowl, and blend well with a hand mixer.

TRANSFER the compound butter mixture onto a large piece of plastic wrap, form into a cylinder about 1 1/2" wide, and refrigerate.

POUND the chicken breasts between two pieces of plastic wrap to a uniform thickness of about 1/3 inch.

MELT two tablespoons butter in a large skillet over high heat.

ADD the chicken as soon as the butter melts.

SAUTE the chicken on both sides until fully cooked and pleasantly browned.

REMOVE the cooked chicken to a platter and continue sautéing the remainder of the chicken.

PREHEAT the oven to 375 degrees.

CUT the chicken into bite sized pieces, about 1 1/2" squares.

PLACE the chicken squares in a single layer on a rimmed cookie sheet.

TOP each piece of chicken with one shrimp.

REMOVE the compound butter from the refrigerator and top the shrimp with a thin slice of the compound butter.

SLICE the mozzarella as thin as possible, and cut into pieces about 1 1/2 inches square.

PLACE a slice of mozzarella on top of the slice of butter.

SPEAR with a toothpick, being sure to pierce the shrimp.

BAKE 10-15 minutes until the butter is completely melted, and the outline of the shrimp is visible through the cheese.

Do-Ahead Tip: The compound butter can be made and frozen weeks in advance. The recipe can be completely assembled two days ahead and refrigerated until ready to bake and serve.

"It is better to go skiing
and think of God,
than to go to church
and think of sport."

~ Fridtjof Nansen

Après Cross Country Skiing Party

Easy Beef Barley Soup

White Seafood Lasagna

Grandma Dott's Green Beans with
Caramelized Onion Butter

White Vegetarian Lasagna

Aunt Sally's Famous Bread Pudding

Mulled Red Wine

Everything

there is to do on the ice or snow can be done in the Adirondacks. If you visit Lake Placid, be sure to go up the elevator of the Olympic ski jump and look down the ramp. You can't even imagine launching yourself on skis down that steep, skinny path. Yet it looks so easy on television!

I'm not fond of winter sports, but I do love the guilty pleasure of a day so snowy that there is no question of venturing out. Adirondack kids wear their pajamas to bed inside out and backwards as a superstitious way to summon a snow day. As a mother, one of my great pleasures was to holler up the stairs "Snow day!" so Sara could stay in bed, which of course she never did. During very bad storms, the roads are closed and all vehicle travel is prohibited. What a perfect time to whip up something wonderful in the kitchen.

My **Easy Beef Barley Soup** is hearty without being too filling, and I think you'll like the two step process of first cooking the beef in a slow cooker for maximum tenderness.

Looking for something different with seafood and pasta? You'll want to try the **White Seafood Lasagna!** The sauce doesn't hide the flavor of the lobster, and when you're using something so expensive, you want to know it's in there! You can also substitute shrimp for the lobster. If you prepare the lasagna more than a day ahead, freeze it so that the pasta doesn't soak up all the sauce and make it dry. Then put it in the oven directly from the freezer. This method also works with the White Vegetarian Lasagna.

Once I told my young niece, Monica, who had volunteered to do the dishes for me that she would need to use some elbow grease to get the lasagna baking dish clean. I went to the market and when I got back, Monica stomped up to me and said, "Aunt Sally, I can't get that pan clean. Where is that elbow grease, anyway?" We still tease her about it to this day.

My grandmother Matilda taught me how to caramelize onions slowly in butter. She came from that wonderful generation of women who lived through the privations of two world wars and the Great Depression, and she could have made old shoe leather taste like a million dollars. **Grandma Dott's Caramelized Onion Butter** can be prepared a few days ahead of time. It can be used in many ways, but my favorite is to put it over fresh green beans steamed until they squeak against your teeth as you test one.

Aunt Sally's Famous Bread Pudding is one of those recipes it pains me to release into the world; like a favored child. It took 24 tries to get it just right. I don't mind sounding like a bread pudding snob when I say that all others fall short of the flavor and texture of this one. There is a wonderful layer of custard on the bottom of the pudding, and the whole recipe only takes ten minutes to assemble. If it comes out of the oven just when your guests are arriving, they will have the pleasure of eating it warm. I never put whipped cream on it, but you can.

The **Mulled Red Wine** is not something you would serve during dinner, but it's a great way to warm up your guests whose noses are red from the cold as they walk in the door. Brrrr.

Easy Beef Barley Soup

1 pound **stew beef**
water
1/2 cup sliced **onion**, plus 1/2 cup chopped **onions**
8 ounces sliced fresh **mushrooms**
1/2 cup chopped **green pepper**
one clove **minced garlic**
2 tablespoons **butter**
6 cups **beef broth**
1/2 teaspoon **salt**
1 teaspoon **sage**
1/2 cup **barley**

PUT stew beef, water and 1/2 cup sliced onions in a slow cooker.

ADD enough water to just cover the beef and onions.

COVER and cook on the low setting 8 hours.

REMOVE the stew beef from the slow cooker.

SHRED the beef.

WHEN ready to make the soup, sauté the chopped onions, mushrooms, green pepper and garlic in butter on medium high heat for about ten minutes.

IN a soup pan, combine the beef broth, salt, sage, barley and shredded beef along with the juices from the slow cooker.

BRING the soup to a boil.

REDUCE the heat to medium low.

COVER and simmer for 20 minutes or until the barley is tender.

Note: If the soup is refrigerated for later use, additional beef broth may be needed as the barley absorbs liquids.

Do-Ahead Tip: This soup can be made two days in advance.

White Seafood Lasagna
reen Beans with Caramelized Onions

White Seafood Lasagna

Serves 9-12

1 cup **butter**
6 cloves minced **garlic**
2 12-ounce cans **evaporated milk**, plus 8 ounces **half-and-half**, equaling 4 cups
2 8-ounce packages **cream cheese**
2 tablespoons **Dijon mustard**
1/2 teaspoon **black pepper**
1 cup, plus 2 tablespoons **Parmesan cheese**
12 **lasagna noodles**
1 pound cooked **lobster meat**, shell pieces and cartilage removed
1 pound cooked **shrimp**, peeled, de-veined, tails removed
8 ounces **cottage cheese**
1 1/2 pounds grated **mozzarella cheese**
1 teaspoon **paprika**

PREHEAT the oven to 350 degrees.

MELT the butter in a saucepan over medium heat.

ADD the minced garlic to the butter and cook for a few minutes.

ADD the evaporated milk, half-and-half, cream cheese, mustard and pepper.

COOK over medium heat, whisking occasionally.

ADD 1 cup Parmesan cheese when the cream cheese is completely melted.

WHISK and cook until the sauce is smooth and the Parmesan cheese has melted.

BOIL the lasagna noodles for exactly ten minutes.

DRAIN the noodles and rinse with cold water.

SPRAY a 12" X 10" X 4" deep baking dish with non-stick spray.

PUT a half cup of the sauce on the bottom of the pan.

LAYER three noodles in the pan, side by side.

RANDOMLY spread a layer of the lobster and shrimp on the noodles, using about 1/3 of the meat for each layer, and reserving a few small pieces of seafood for the top.

SCATTER about a tablespoon of cottage cheese over each noodle.

ADD a layer of the mozzarella cheese, using about 1/3 of the cheese for each layer.

LADLE sauce over the top of this layer, using 1/3 cup of the sauce for each noodle.

REPEAT the layers. There will be a total of four layers of noodles and three layers of filling.

SPREAD 1 cup of the sauce on the top layer of noodles.

SPRINKLE with two tablespoons Parmesan cheese and the paprika.

TOP with the reserved pieces of the seafood.

COVER with foil, sealing the edges.

BAKE 45 minutes to an hour until the edges are bubbling, or until the center registers 160 degrees with a quick tip thermometer.

IMPORTANT!!! Allow this to sit for at least ten minutes to allow the ingredients to set before cutting.

Note: There will be leftover sauce which you can use on pasta, or it can be frozen for use in the next lasagna.

Do-Ahead Tip: This lasagna can be made weeks in advance and frozen. Bake, covered, for 2 1/2 to 3 hours if frozen. The lasagna can also be made the day before and refrigerated.

Grandma Dott's Green Beans with Caramelized Onion Butter

Serves 8

1 large **onion**, diced
3/4 cup **butter**
2 pounds **fresh whole green beans**
salt and **pepper**, optional

PUT the onions in a small sauté pan with the butter.

COOK over medium low heat for at least an hour, stirring occasionally.

WHEN done, the onions will be golden brown.

STEAM or boil the green beans until tender crisp.

ADD salt and pepper to taste, if desired.

DRAIN and top with the hot onion butter.

SERVE immediately.

Do-Ahead Tip: Prepare the onion butter up to two days in advance and refrigerate, or freeze it, until ready to use. The beans can be steamed earlier in the day and reheated when ready to serve.

White Vegetarian Lasagna

Serves 9-12

- 1 cup **butter**
- 6 cloves minced **garlic**
- 2 12-ounce cans **evaporated milk**, plus 8 ounces **half-and-half**, equaling 4 cups
- 2 8-ounce packages **cream cheese**
- 2 tablespoon **Dijon mustard**
- 1/2 teaspoon **black pepper**
- 1 cup, plus 2 tablespoons **Parmesan cheese**
- 12 **lasagna noodles**
- 1 slivered **red pepper**
- 3 **carrots**, peeled and cut into thick shreds
- 1 medium sliced **zucchini**, 1/2" thick
- 1 medium sliced **yellow squash**, 1/2" thick
- 8 ounces fresh sliced **mushrooms**
- 1/2 pound **asparagus**, cut into 1" pieces
- 8 ounces **cottage cheese**
- 1 1/2 pounds grated **mozzarella cheese**
- 1 teaspoon **paprika**

PREHEAT the oven to 350 degrees.

SAUTE the mushrooms in 2 tablespoons butter over medium heat until tender.

SET aside.

PREPARE the raw vegetables and set aside.

MELT 1/2 cup butter in a saucepan over medium heat.

ADD the minced garlic to the butter and cook for a few minutes.

ADD the evaporated milk, half-and-half, cream cheese, mustard and pepper.

COOK over medium heat, whisking occasionally.

ADD 1 cup Parmesan cheese.

WHISK and cook until the sauce is smooth and the Parmesan cheese has melted.

BOIL the lasagna noodles for exactly ten minutes.

DRAIN the noodles and rinse with cold water.

SPRAY a 12" X 10" X 4" deep baking dish with non-stick spray.

PUT a half cup of the sauce on the bottom of the pan.

LAYER three noodles in the pan, side by side.

RANDOMLY spread a layer of the vegetables, using about 1/3 of each vegetable for each layer.

SCATTER about a tablespoon of cottage cheese on each noodle.

ADD a layer of the mozzarella cheese, using about 1/3 of the cheese for each layer.

LADLE sauce over the top of this layer, using 1/3 cup of the sauce for each noodle.

REPEAT the layers. There will be a total of four layers of noodles and three layers of filling.

SPREAD 1 cup of the sauce on the top layer of noodles.

SPRINKLE with two tablespoons Parmesan cheese and the paprika.

COVER with foil, sealing the edges.

BAKE 45 minutes to one hour until the edges are bubbling, or until the center registers 160 degrees with a quick tip thermometer.

IMPORTANT!!! Allow this to sit for at least ten minutes to allow the ingredients to set before cutting.

Note: There will be leftover sauce which you can use on pasta, or it can be frozen for use in the next lasagna.

Do-Ahead Tip: This lasagna can be made weeks in advance and frozen. Bake, covered, for 2 1/2 to 3 hours if frozen. The lasagna can also be made the day before and refrigerated.

Aunt Sally's Famous Bread Pudding

Serves 10-12

2 cups **sugar**
1 cup **butter**
3 cups **water**
6 **eggs**
2 12-ounce cans **evaporated milk**
2 teaspoons **vanilla**
ground **cinnamon**
1 16-ounce loaf **cinnamon raisin swirl bread**,
    using all but three slices of the loaf

PREHEAT the oven to 350 degrees.

HEAT the butter, sugar and water in a sauce pan, stirring occasionally until the butter has melted.

WHISK together the eggs, evaporated milk and vanilla in a mixing bowl.

COAT a 12"X10"X4" deep glass baking dish with non-stick cooking spray.

BREAK the slices of cinnamon raisin bread into quarter-sized pieces, layering on the bottom of the glass dish.

STIR the melted butter mixture into the egg mixture, continuing to stir while pouring.

POUR the combined mixture over the bread layer, pushing the bread pieces down into the liquid to ensure all the bread is thoroughly moistened.

LIGHTLY sprinkle the top with cinnamon.

BAKE 55 minutes.

TEST for doneness. It will puff up, particularly in the middle, but still be somewhat jiggly.

SERVE when cool, or refrigerate.

Do-Ahead Tip: *This recipe can be made five days in advance. Cover and refrigerate.*

Mulled Red Wine

Serves 6

750 ml bottle **full bodied red wine** such as Merlot
2 **cinnamon sticks**, broken in half
1 **star anise**
2 **whole cloves**
1 quarter sized piece **fresh ginger**
1 **orange**, unpeeled, cut into 6 pieces
1/2 cup **sugar**
1/4 cup **brandy**, optional

COMBINE all the ingredients in a saucepan.

SIMMER without boiling until thoroughly heated.

STRAIN and transfer to a thermal carafe or pump pot to keep hot while serving.

Do-Ahead Tip: *This recipe can be made a day in advance, refrigerated, and reheated before serving.*

Aunt Sally's Famous Bread Pudding

"I am still convinced that a good, simple, homemade cookie is preferable to all the store-bought cookies one can find."

~ James Beard

Adirondack Christmas Cookie Swap

Gail's Buckeye Balls

Aunt Evelyn's Molasses Cookies

Aunt Evelyn's Date Swirl Cookies

Cranberry Un-Biscotti

Grandma Dott's Raisin Nut Tarts

Aunt Evelyn's Spritz Cookies

Grandma Dott's Vienna Bars

Chocolate Dipped Orange Cookies

Jelly Filled Sugar Cookies

Emergency Reese's Mini Brownies

Nothing says "I love you" better than homemade cookies, because cookies are never a dietary necessity, just a luxury! Every family has their favorites, and in our house, Sara always wants the humble **"Not Flat" Chocolate Chip Cookies.** So we make those at Christmas time, too. The recipe can be found on page 51.

This special collection of recipes, most from the recipe boxes of beloved relatives, includes the ones I always make during the Christmas season. The temporary isolation created by a big snowfall always sends me to the kitchen to make cookies.

Cookie swaps are not unique to the Adirondacks, but they are a wonderful way to have a varied assortment of cookies to enjoy during the holidays with the luxury of not having to do all the work yourself. If you are inviting eight people, have each person bring ten dozen of just one kind of cookie, making sure ahead of time that no two people are baking the same cookie. Each person takes home a dozen of each kind, eight dozen in all, and there are enough left over for sampling during the cookie exchange. Most cookies keep at least a week in a tightly closed tin, and the ones that don't can be frozen. Sharing the recipes is fun, so ask your friends ahead of time to bring copies of their recipes to exchange.

The dough for many of these recipes can be frozen ahead of time for busy Christmas season baking, which I prefer over freezing baked cookies. Thaw the dough when you are ready and you'll have freshly baked cookies in minutes! If you have formed your cookies prior to freezing, put them directly from the freezer into a preheated oven.

For many years, my sisters, Gail and Jacquie, and I had an annual "cookie day". We spent a whole weekend together whipping up twenty different kinds of cookies, so we could divide the spoils, and give them away to friends and co-workers! One year Jacquie's active young boys were driving her crazy because they were bored. Determined to keep baking, she dumped a five pound bag of flour in the middle of her kitchen floor and they played in it with their toy trucks for hours. Gail and I couldn't believe it! Years later, I recalled that fun mess and I had Sara rolling cookies in a cloud of confectioner's sugar when she was just a toddler. I have a photo of her and half the kitchen covered in powdered sugar. Don't miss the opportunity for those moments.

We can't remember where we got this recipe, but my sisters and I call them **Gail's Buckeye Balls** because Gail is always the one who gets the annual pleasure of making them. They're not difficult; just tedious when making thousands of them, as Gail always does. With a little planning, you can use the chocolate leftover from the Buckeye Balls to dip the **Chocolate Dipped Orange Cookies** in. Orange and chocolate are a classic combination that never disappoints, and these cookies are no exception! The nice thing about slice and bake recipes is that you can make just a few cookies if you want to.

It's not officially the Christmas season until my mother makes **Grandma Dott's Raisin Nut Tarts** for the whole family. It's the only time of year we engage in "jelly bean counting". We all want to be sure that we get our fair share of the batch! Mom freezes the raw pie crust dough in November, so that assembly in busy December will be easier. My grandmother made them for over seventy years. She said she got the recipe from a very old German woman, who was born in the early 1800's. Mom took over the task of making them when Gram got too old, and someday it will be my turn to make them every Christmas, but I'm in no rush.

Grandma Dott's Vienna Bars recipe also comes from my grandmother, one source of my entrepreneurial genes. In the 1930's she made fancy hats and had a showroom in her front parlor. In the summer, she would sell German bearded irises from her huge garden. Gram's been gone over twenty years but every so often I run across someone who remembers the "iris lady". I never thought to ask Gram why she called them Vienna bars, but I'll bet it was a great story.

Aunt Evelyn was actually the aunt of my ex-husband. When we divorced, I told him he could have the boat, but that I was keeping Aunt Evelyn. **Aunt Evelyn's Date Swirl Cookies** are a bit of work so I only make them once a year, but that makes them even more special.

The half cup of cornstarch in **Aunt Evelyn's Spritz Cookies** sounds weird, but try them anyway. The cornstarch gives the cookies a wonderful crispness that is hard to describe. Be sure to let these cookies brown at the edges. It will make all the difference in their flavor.

Aunt Evelyn was one of the best cooks I have known, and she was the quintessential 'hostess with the mostess'. Her elegant entertaining seemed effortless, and every dinner party was an event. In the winter, she muddled the Manhattans when she heard the crunch of our tires on the snow and handed the drinks to us right after taking our coats. Most everything I know about entertaining, I learned from her.

If the idea of a molasses sugar cookie doesn't excite you, try **Aunt Evelyn's Molasses Cookies** recipe. Pulling them from the oven right when cracks develop means that the edges will be crispy and the centers soft, yet chewy. I like to sit all by myself when I am eating the first cookie out of the oven so that I can be as one with it and my memories of Aunt Evelyn. I insert an ornament hanger into another cookie, let it cool, and hang it from the Christmas tree. I like to think she would have been happy to be remembered in this way. Aunt Evelyn had a covered china casserole dish on her kitchen table that she used as a cookie jar. After she got cancer, I used the cookie jar as a barometer for how she was feeling, because she refused to complain. When she had a bad day, it was empty. Of such bittersweet memories are lives made.

When your child announces at 9 p.m. that she has volunteered you to provide the snack for the class holiday party the next day, let the **Emergency Reese's Mini Brownies** come to the rescue. When Sara was young, I kept a box of brownie mix and a bag of miniature peanut butter cups hidden in the back of the cupboard for just such occasions! The mini brownies are ready in no time and kids of all ages love them. Don't forget to get the kids to help. Even toddlers can remove the wrappers from the peanut butter cups, or stir the batter. You're also whipping up memories that will last a lifetime!

Gail's Buckeye Balls

Makes 200

16 ounces **creamy peanut butter**
16 ounces **extra crunchy peanut butter**
1 pound **butter** at room temperature
3 pounds **confectioner's sugar**
3 tablespoons **vanilla**
24 ounces **semi-sweet chocolate chips**
1/2 bar of **paraffin wax**, broken into pieces
metal turkey **skewers**

PUT the peanut butters, butter, sugar and vanilla into a very large bowl. Start mixing with a wooden spoon but finish using the hands. The dough is thick, but a heavy duty mixer can handle mixing the dough.

FORM the dough into 1" balls, place on a cookie sheet covered with plastic wrap.

COVER with plastic wrap.

REFRIGERATE for several hours or overnight, or freeze.

WHEN ready to dip the balls, put the chocolate and wax into a slow cooker set on low.

WHILE melting, stir to blend the chocolate and wax.

USING metal turkey skewers, spear one ball at a time, going about half an inch deep into the ball with the skewer.

DIP the balls into the chocolate and place the chocolate-covered ball onto a plastic wrap covered cookie sheet.

AFTER removing the skewer, use the skewer to cover the little hole with additional chocolate.

MAKE sure the balls do not touch each other.

REFRIGERATE until the chocolate is hard and then put the balls in air tight containers. It is okay to stack them at this point.

STORE in the refrigerator.

Optional: Use milk chocolate chips to achieve a flavor closest to Reese's peanut butter cups.

Do-Ahead Tip: These can be made three weeks in advance.

Aunt Evelyn's Molasses Cookies

Makes 5 dozen

1 1/2 cups solid **shortening**
2 cups **sugar**
1/2 cup **molasses**
2 **eggs**
4 cups **flour**
4 teaspoons **baking soda**
1 teaspoon **ground cloves**
1 teaspoon **ground ginger**
2 teaspoons **ground cinnamon**
1 teaspoon **salt**
sugar for coating

PREHEAT the oven to 375 degrees.

MELT and cool the shortening.

COMBINE the cooled shortening, sugar, molasses and eggs.

BEAT with a hand mixer until well mixed.

ADD the remaining ingredients and mix into a dough.

CHILL the dough a couple of hours.

FORM portions of the dough into 1 1/4" balls.

ROLL the balls in granulated sugar.

PLACE the sugared balls 2" apart on an ungreased cookie sheet.

BAKE 8-10 minutes, until the cookies begin to crack around the edges. Baking longer will result in a crispier cookie.

ALLOW to cool before removing from the cookie sheet.

Do-Ahead Tip: *The dough can be made, formed into balls (or not) and frozen a month in advance. These cookies can be made a week in advance. Store in an airtight container.*

Aunt Evelyn's Date Swirl Cookies

Makes 3 dozen

Dough

2 cups **flour**
1 cup **brown sugar**
1/2 cup **butter**
1 tablespoon **milk**
1 tablespoon **vanilla**
1/2 teaspoon **baking soda**
1/2 teaspoon **baking powder**
dash **salt**
1 **egg**

COMBINE all the ingredients in a large bowl.

BEAT at medium speed with a hand mixer for three minutes.

FORM a disk of the dough, cover with plastic wrap and refrigerate several hours or until the next day.

Filling

2 1/2 cups whole, pitted **dates**, finely chopped
1/2 cup **sugar**
1/2 cup **orange juice**
1 teaspoon grated **orange peel**
dash **salt**
1 cup **walnuts or pecans**, chopped fine

PLACE all the ingredients, **except** the walnuts, in a small sauce pan.

BRING to a boil over medium heat, stirring occasionally.

REDUCE the heat to a simmer and cook two minutes or until most of the liquid has been absorbed.

STIR the chopped nuts into the filling.

COOL to room temperature before proceeding to assembly. Do not refrigerate the filling.

Assembly

HEAVILY flour a sheet of waxed paper or parchment. Place half the dough disk on the floured paper.

FLOUR the top of the dough.

ROLL out a 12"x 9" rectangle using a floured rolling pin.

SPREAD half the filling evenly over the dough, close to the edges.

ROLL the dough up in jelly roll fashion.

WRAP the dough roll in plastic wrap.

REPEAT with the other half of the dough.

FREEZE the rolls overnight.

Baking

PREHEAT the oven to 375 degrees.

SLICE each roll into 1/3" thick pieces using a sharp knife. To get a puffy, softer cookie, make 1/2" cuts. For a crispy cookie, make 1/4" cuts.

PLACE the slices on a cookie sheet lined with parchment paper.

BAKE 10 minutes until lightly browned and puffed up.

COOL 5 minutes then loosen with a spatula and allow to cool on the parchment.

> **Note:** If stacking, place a sheet of parchment paper between the layers. Otherwise, the cookies will stick together.

> **Do-Ahead Tip:** Once assembled, the dough rolls may be frozen for baking at a future date.

Cranberry Un-Biscotti

Makes 24 pieces

1 1/2 cups **sugar**
1/2 cup **butter**
2 **eggs**
1/2 teaspoon **vanilla**
2 1/2 cups **flour**
1 teaspoon **baking powder**
1/2 teaspoon **salt**
1 1/2 cups **dried cranberries**
1 **egg white**
sliced almonds, optional

PREHEAT the oven to 350 degrees.

CREAM the sugar, butter, eggs and vanilla with a hand mixer.

ADD the flour, baking powder, salt and cranberries to the creamed mixture.

CONTINUE mixing until completely blended.

DIVIDE the dough in two equal portions.

PUT each half on parchment paper and form into logs about 10" long and 2" in diameter. Slightly flatten the logs.

BRUSH the tops of the logs with one egg white, beaten until foamy.

SPRINKLE with sliced almonds, if desired.

BAKE 33 minutes, or until nicely browned on top. A toothpick, when inserted, will come out clean when the log is done.

COOL completely.

SLICE into 1" slices, and serve.

Optional: Dip the baked slices in melted chocolate, if desired.

Note: To make this into "real" biscotti, make half inch slices, turn them on their sides, and return to the oven for ten minutes. Turn the slices over and bake five minutes longer. They will dry out and get crunchy.

Do-Ahead Tip: This recipe can be made a week in advance. Store the slices in an airtight container. The raw dough can be made and frozen months in advance, then thawed and baked.

Grandma Dott's Raisin Nut Tarts

Makes 24 tarts

2 **pie crusts**
2 cups **sugar**
2/3 cup softened **butter**
8 tablespoons **milk**
4 **eggs**
2 cups chopped **walnuts**
2 cups **raisins**

PREHEAT the oven to 350 degrees.

ROLL out the crusts and cut into 4" circles.

FIT the cut circles into cupcake tins.

COMBINE the sugar, softened butter, milk and eggs in a mixing bowl.

BEAT well with an hand mixer.

ADD the walnuts and raisins to the egg mixture.

MIX to combine well.

POUR 1/4 cup of the filling into each pie crust shell.

BAKE 25-30 minutes or until the outside of the pie crust is light golden brown.

Do-Ahead Tip: These tarts can be made two weeks in advance. Store in an airtight container.

Aunt Evelyn's Spritz Cookies

Makes 3-4 dozen

2 cups **butter** at room temperature
1 cup **sugar**
1 **egg**
1 teaspoon **vanilla**
3 1/2 cups **flour**
1/2 cup **cornstarch**

PREHEAT the oven to 350 degrees.

CREAM the sugar and butter using a hand mixer.

BEAT the egg and vanilla into the creamed mixture.

ADD the flour and cornstarch.

MIX just until blended.

USING a spritz press or a pastry bag with an Ateco tip #827, press the dough onto ungreased cookie sheets into any desired shape such as a 2 1/2" wreath.

DECORATE with sprinkles or colored sugar, if desired.

BAKE 12-15 minutes or until golden brown on the edges and the bottom.

Do-Ahead Tip: The dough can be made and frozen three months in advance. The cookies can be made two weeks in advance. Store in an airtight container.

137

Grandma Dott's Vienna Bars

Makes 24 bars

Crust

1 cup **butter**
1/2 cup **sugar**
2 **egg yolks**
dash **salt**
2 1/2 cups **flour**

PREHEAT the oven to 350 degrees.
CREAM the butter, sugar and egg yolks.
ADD the salt and flour.
COMBINE with a hand mixer.
PAT the dough into a 13" X 9" pan.
BAKE 15-20 minutes until lightly browned.
FILL with preserves and top with meringue as follows.

Filling

1 10-ounce jar **raspberry preserves**

STIR in a bowl.
SPREAD on the top of the baked crust.

Meringue Topping

4 **egg whites**
1 cup **sugar**
2 cups finely chopped **pecans** or **walnuts**

BEAT the egg whites until stiff.
FOLD the sugar and nuts into the stiff egg whites.
SPREAD the meringue topping evenly over the preserves.
RETURN to the oven and bake 25 minutes until lightly browned.
IMMEDIATELY score the top with a knife when removed from the oven to indicate where to cut the bars later. This will help keep the meringue intact while cutting.
COOL completely and slice along the scored lines.

Do-Ahead Tip: *These bars can be made a week in advance. Store in an airtight container.*

Aunt Evelyn's Date Swirl Cookies
Grandma Dott's Raisin Nut Tarts
Gail's Buckeye Balls
Aunt Evelyn's Molasses Cookies
Cranberry Un-Biscotti
Aunt Evelyn's Spritz Cookies
Chocolate Dipped Orange Cookies

Chocolate Dipped Orange Cookies

Makes 5 dozen

11 tablespoons **butter**
1 **egg**
4 teaspoons **milk**
1 teaspoon **vanilla**
2 teaspoons **grated orange rind**
2 cups **flour**
1 teaspoon **baking powder**
1/2 teaspoon **salt**
24 ounces **semi-sweet chocolate chips**
1/2 bar of **paraffin wax**, broken into pieces

CREAM the butter, egg, milk, vanilla and orange rind with a hand mixer.

ADD the flour, baking powder and salt, continuing to mix until well blended.

DIVIDE the dough into two equal pieces. The cookies will double in size when baked.

FORM each piece into an oval shaped log about 8" long, and cover with plastic wrap.

FREEZE.

WHEN ready to bake, preheat the oven to 375 degrees.

SLICE the dough into 1/4" slices.

PLACE 2" apart on an ungreased cookie sheet.

BAKE 8-10 minutes until the edges are lightly browned.

COOL 10 minutes and loosen the cookies with a spatula.

CAREFULLY transfer the cookies to wire racks to finish cooling.

WHEN ready to dip the cookies, put the chocolate and wax into a slow cooker set on low.

WHILE melting, stir to blend the chocolate and wax.

DIP one end of the cookie into the melted chocolate.

PLACE each dipped cookie on a plastic wrap lined cookie sheet.

Note: After dipping in chocolate, the cookies can be refrigerated to speed up the firming of the chocolate.

Do-Ahead Tip: The dough MUST be frozen prior to slicing and baking. The dough can be made and frozen three months in advance.

Jelly Filled Sugar Cookies

Makes 3 dozen

1 cup **butter**
2 cups **sugar**
2 **eggs**
4 tablespoons **milk**
1 teaspoon **vanilla**
3 1/2 cups **flour**
4 teaspoons **baking powder**
1 teaspoon **salt**
raspberry jelly

PREHEAT the oven to 375 degrees.

CREAM the butter, sugar, eggs, milk and vanilla with a hand mixer.

ADD the flour, baking powder and salt, continuing to mix until well blended.

DROP rounded teaspoons of dough onto an ungreased cookie sheet, 3' apart.

MAKE an indentation in the middle of each cookie with the floured end of a wooden spoon.

FILL with jelly.

BAKE 10 minutes or until light golden brown at edges.

Do-Ahead Tip: *The raw dough can be made weeks in advance and frozen. Thaw in the refrigerator overnight.*

Gail's Buckeye Balls

Emergency Reese's Mini Brownies

Makes 36

1 box **Duncan Hines brownie mix**
36 **miniature Reese's peanut butter cups**

PREHEAT the oven to 350 degrees.

SPRAY mini-muffin pans with baking spray.

MIX the brownies according to package directions.

FILL the muffin cups 2/3 full.

REMOVE the wrapping from the peanut butter cups.

PRESS a mini peanut butter cup into the batter of each muffin cup, leaving 1/8" of the peanut butter cup above the level of the batter. Do not submerge it in the batter. The batter should then be just below the rim of the muffin cup.

BAKE 13 minutes.

COOL for 10-15 minutes.

CAREFULLY remove the brownies from the mini-muffin pan to finish cooling.

Do-Ahead Tip: *These can be made three days in advance if stored in an airtight container.*

"One of the most glorious messes
in the world
is the mess created in the living room
on Christmas day.
Don't clean it up too quickly."

~ Andy Rooney

Make-Ahead Christmas Morning Brunch

Fresh Fruit Salad

Cheddar Sausage Breakfast Strata

Vegetarian Breakfast Strata

Pumpkin Walnut Bread

Amanda's Frozen Fruit Smoothies

A white Christmas in the Adirondacks is

generally a given, but even if you don't have snow at your house, it's a short trip to the mountains to find some. Christmas Eve three years ago, we got two feet of snow and it was just like being inside one of those glass snow globes. It's already a tradition in our family to say "Remember that year we got two feet of snow on Christmas Eve?" My friend Cindy had just moved here from Georgia that week and was more than a little nervous when she asked, "Does this happen often?"

And I can't explain it, but if you go out into the woods just after a big snowfall, it sounds different than at other times. The occasional "pouf" of snow falling from a tree limb punctuates a wonderful nothingness of true silence.

It's natural for caterers to design do-ahead recipes, but never more so than during the Christmas season. That's when we're really busy, and we feel terribly guilty for not feeding our own families as well as we do our clients. Of such anguish was this menu conceived! A special family memory at our house is of Holly, our first dachshund. She and Sara grew up together, and Holly loved Christmas. She would wait until the piles of discarded wrapping paper were about a foot deep, and then she would tunnel through them, looking for the doggy treats she knew Sara had hidden for her.

Around here Amanda is the "smoothie queen" and she discovered that **Frozen Fruit Smoothies** can be made a month ahead of time and frozen. Then overnight in the refrigerator, or a mere two minutes in the microwave, and some vigorous stirring gives you a quick breakfast treat. Using frozen berries eliminates the need to add ice and makes a better flavored smoothie.

145

To make the **Cheddar Sausage Breakfast Strata** assembly on Christmas Eve a twenty minute process, the sausage for the strata can be cooked, crumbled, and frozen a week or two in advance. After you prepare the strata, let it sit in the refrigerator overnight, and on Christmas morning, you pop the strata in the oven and are able to enjoy your family while waiting for the timer to go off.

My **Fresh Fruit Salad** always gets rave reviews, with people asking - "where do you buy your fruit?" The answer is: Everywhere! It usually takes visits to more than one market to find good quality fruit, especially in the winter. If you can't find decent grapes or cantaloupe or whichever fruit, just leave it out rather than compromise the whole salad. The next thing of key importance for a fruit salad, when you are making it the night before, is to store each kind of fruit separately in 'zip' bags. This prevents the enzymes of each fruit from affecting the others. When it's time to serve the fruit, use a glass punch bowl, layering the fruits over and over again until the bowl is full. Be careful not to have any excess juices from the fruits going into the bowl or all the fruits will taste the same. Then top off your fruit salad with blackberries or blueberries for beautiful color contrast, and you'll have a masterpiece.

Another recipe from Gert O'Brien is the **Pumpkin Walnut Bread**. It's good, and so easy! Be sure to leave the walnuts in large pieces so that they announce themselves and add a crunch. If you are going to freeze the bread ahead of time, don't add the glaze until the day before you are ready to serve it.

Merry Christmas! Now put your feet up!

Fresh Fruit Salad

1. Be prepared to go to more than one vendor or store to purchase fruit. Don't buy anything that doesn't look good. It's better to have guests wishing for strawberries than to serve them sour ones.

2. To fill a punch bowl, and have enough fruit remaining for a refill, use the following fruits, prepared as indicated:

   - 1/2 seedless watermelon, cut into melon balls
   - 1 cantaloupe, cut into melon balls
   - 1 honeydew, cut into melon balls
   - 1 pineapple, cubed
   - 1 pound red grapes
   - 1 pound green grapes
   - 5 kiwi, peeled and sliced
   - 2 ripe mangoes, peeled and cubed
   - 1 star fruit, sliced
   - 1 quart strawberries, stemmed and halved
   - 1/2 pound cherries
   - 1 small ripe papaya, peeled and cubed
   - 1 pint blackberries or blueberries, to put on top

3. Leave small fruits whole. Don't cut fruit so small that it can't be identified.

4. Don't use apples, pears or or bananas in fresh fruit salads - they brown quickly and are unattractive.

5. Fruit can be cut up the night before serving it. It's important to store each kind of fruit separately in 'zip' bags. The enzymes of different fruits speed up the ripening/decaying of other fruits. Just before serving the fruit salad, layer it into a pretty glass bowl, repeating layers until the bowl is filled. Don't add any accumulated fruit juices to the bowl, as these juices will make all the fruits taste the same.

6. Top the fruit salad with dark blue fruits, such as blackberries or blueberries. These are a wonderful contrast to the colors of the other fruits. They look especially pretty next to chunks of mango or papaya. If there are cherries in the salad, remind guests they need to watch for pits.

Cheddar Sausage Breakfast Strata
Fresh Fruit Salad

Cheddar Sausage
Breakfast Strata

Serves 10

8 slices fresh **white bread**
2 pounds bulk **breakfast sausage**
2 cups shredded **extra sharp cheddar cheese**
6 **eggs**
1/2 teaspoon **dry mustard**
1/8 teaspoon **Tabasco**
3 cups **milk** (skim will work)
1/2 teaspoon **Beau Monde Seasoning**
1/2 teaspoon each **salt** and **pepper**, or to taste

GREASE a 13"x9" deep baking dish.

CUT the bread into small cubes, leaving the crusts on.

COOK and drain the sausage. Crumble when cool.

LAYER the bread cubes, then the crumbled sausage and finally the cheese in the baking dish.

BLEND the eggs, dry mustard, Tabasco, milk, Beau Monde Seasoning, salt and pepper with a hand mixer.

POUR this mixture over the bread, sausage and cheese making sure the bread is evenly moistened.

COVER and refrigerate overnight.

IN the morning, preheat the oven to 325 degrees.

BAKE, uncovered, an hour or until there is a nice browning and the center has visible puffing.

SERVE while hot.

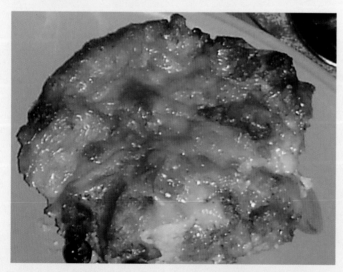

Note: The strata must be prepared the night before baking.

Do-Ahead Tip: The sausage can be cooked ahead and frozen. Thaw when ready to prepare the recipe.

Vegetarian
Breakfast Strata

Serves 10

8 slices fresh **white bread**
1 medium **zucchini**, 1/4" thick slices
1 **red bell pepper**, slivered
1 bunch **broccoli**, cut into florets, optional
2 cups shredded **extra sharp cheddar cheese**
6 **eggs**
1/2 teaspoon **dry mustard**
1/8 teaspoon **Tabasco**
3 cups **milk** (skim will work)
1/2 teaspoon **Beau Monde Seasoning**
1/2 teaspoon each **salt** and **pepper**, or to taste

GREASE a 13"x9" deep baking dish.

CUT the bread into small cubes, leaving the crusts on.

SAUTE the zucchini and peppers briefly over high heat in a frying pan.

LAYER the bread cubes, then the sautéed vegetables including the raw broccoli, if desired, and finally the cheese in the baking dish.

BLEND the eggs, dry mustard, Tabasco, milk, Beau Monde Seasoning, salt and pepper with a hand mixer.

POUR this mixture over the bread, vegetables and cheese making sure the bread is evenly moistened.

COVER and refrigerate overnight.

IN the morning, preheat the oven to 325 degrees.

BAKE, uncovered, an hour or until there is a nice browning and the center has visible puffing.

SERVE while hot.

Note: *The strata must be prepared the night before baking.*

Do-Ahead Tip: *The vegetables can be prepared and stored individually in 'zip' bags two days in advance.*

Pumpkin Walnut Bread

Makes 2 large loaves or 5 mini loaves

1 cup **oil**
3 **eggs**
2 cups **sugar**
1 15-ounce can **plain pumpkin**
1/2 teaspoon **salt**
1 teaspoon **baking soda**
2 teaspoons **baking powder**
1 teaspoon **cinnamon**
1 teaspoon **nutmeg**
1/4 teaspoon **ground cloves**
3 cups **flour**
3/4 cup broken **walnuts**
softened **butter**

PREHEAT the oven to 325 degrees.

CREAM the oil, eggs and sugar using a hand mixer.

ADD the remaining ingredients, except butter, stirring until combined.

GREASE and flour two large loaf pans or five mini-loaf pans.

BAKE one hour, or until a toothpick inserted in the center comes out clean.

WHEN the bread comes out of the oven, brush the top with softened butter and allow to cool completely.

GLAZE using the following recipe.

ALLOW the glaze to set before slicing.

Glaze

1 cup **confectioner's sugar**
1/4 teaspoon **vanilla**
1 tablespoon **milk**

COMBINE all the ingredients.

STIR until the sugar is completely dissolved and the glaze is a smooth consistency.

Do-Ahead Tip: *This pumpkin bread can be made three days in advance. It can be baked and frozen without the glaze weeks ahead. Thaw overnight in the refrigerator and glaze before serving.*

Amanda's Frozen Fruit Smoothies

Makes 3 10-ounce drinks

1 **banana**, 2 if they are small
12 large **frozen strawberries**, unsweetened
1/3 cup **frozen blueberries**, unsweetened
1 cup **skim milk**
1/3 cup **orange juice**
1 teaspoon **vanilla extract**
1/8 cup **sugar**, optional
1/8 cup **frozen juice concentrate**, any flavor, optional

COMBINE all the ingredients in a blender, putting the banana(s) in first. Blend until the mixture is a uniform consistency.

Do-Ahead Tip: *This mixture can be prepared and frozen two weeks in advance. Freeze it in 8 ounce containers. When ready to use, microwave the frozen smoothie 2-3 minutes on defrost and stir vigorously.*

Frozen Fruit Smoothies and Pumpkin Walnut Bread

Acknowledgements

Ben Moore
BRM Photography
http://home.earthlink.net/~brmphotovideo
Front cover photo

Gerry Lemmo
www.gerrylemmo.com
518-793-3058
Photography ©2007 Gerry Lemmo. All rights reserved.
Adirondack photos:
  Black bear in ferns - The Whitney Area, Long Lake ...page IX
  Common merganser family - Little Tupper Lake...page XII
  Mossy rocks in Tripp Lake Brook – Warrensburg...page 13
  Eastern chipmunk eating crab apple - Glens Falls...page 23
  White-tailed deer fawn – Salem...page 37
  Male pileated woodpecker at nest – Ticonderoga...page 53
  Poplar Point sunset - Raquette Lake...page 65
  Maple leaf on log cabin - Stony Creek...page 79
  Polar bear hot air balloon - Adirondack Balloon Festival -
      Queensbury...page 84
  Stewart Brook reflections - Lake Luzerne...page 93
  Snowshoeing on Tongue Mt. - Lake George...page 113
  Adirondack chairs at The Adirondack Visitor Interpretive Center -
      Paul Smiths...page 125
  Christmas sleigh – Queensbury...page 143
  Rustic barn detail – Jay...page XIV

Sally Longo
Aunt Sally's Catering
sjlongo@msn.com
www.adkcookbook.com
518-798-9598
Food styling
Food photography
Iris at Yaddo Photo .... Page 1
Photo on page 91 taken at the Carpenter family farm
Photos on pages 118 & 139 taken at the LaCabanna Lodge, access
    courtesy of Rob & Donna Slack

Melony Longhitano
A Lasting Impression Florist
www.alastimp.com
518-743-0415
All floral arrangements shown in photos

Christian Salmonsen, Graphic Designer
New York Press & Graphics
www.nypressandgraphics.com
Cover design

Gail Wilty, Executive Operations Manager
New York Press & Graphics
www.nypressandgraphics.com
Printer of this book

Ed Gazel, Videographer
518-543-6903
Photo on page 74

Valerie Nusskern
Cosmetic Junkies
www.cosmeticjunkies.com
Hair & makeup for front cover photo

Nancy Murtha
Pagination, graphic design, photography and text editing

All dishware, tablecloths and flatware privately owned by Sally Longo except as follows:
   Pottery dinner plates, pages 87 & 91, from the private collection of June Carey
   French pottery plates, pages 98, 108 & 137, from the private collection of Judy Johnson
   Tablecloths, pages 36, 73 & 76 from the private collection of Judy Johnson

**All the food in photographs is shown exactly as it looked when prepared.
No food styling tools, such as glycerin, were used to enhance any of the food in the photos.**

Local Resources and Vendors

ABC Restaurant Equipment & Supply
28 Elm Street Glens Falls, NY 12801   518-793-3456
www.abcofglensfalls.com
Everything for the aspiring chef, from Fiestaware for the table to residential cooking equipment, stoves, refrigerators, dishwashers, and all things in between. "Our mission is YOUR success." Friendly owner Rick Burr will order it if he doesn't have it in stock.

A Lasting Impression Florist
Queensbury, NY 12804   518-743-0415
www.alastimp.com
From a small arrangement to a complete Adirondack wedding, owner Melony Longhitano will translate your vision into flowers.

Allerdice Rent-All
221 West Circular, Saratoga, NY 12866   518-584-1412
www.allerdicepartyrentall.com
If you're having a party, they've got what you need. Everything from tents to china, linens, glassware, and five kinds of chairs.

Bobby Dick & the Sundowners
518-793-1099
www.bobbydick.com
The premiere local band to get your party started.

Cooper's Cave Brewery
Corner Dix & Sagamore Streets, Glens Falls, NY 12801   518-792-0007
www.cooperscaveale.com
Micro-brew beers and homemade ice cream.

Davidson Brothers Restaurant & Brewery
184 Glen Street, Glens Falls, NY 12801   518-743-9026
www.davidsonbrothers.com
You can have their micro-brew beer delivered and set up on tap for your party. Try their Dacker Ale!

Dobert's Dairy
68 Third Street, Glens Falls, NY 12801   518-792-3415
www.doberts.com
Anything dairy, frozen, flat sheets of puff pastry, canned & bagged goods, bread crumbs, rice, Belgian Waffle mix. Try their holiday ice cream flavors such as pumpkin, gingerbread, and peppermint stick.

Double A Provisions
64 Main Street, Queensbury, NY 12804   518-792-2494
www.doubleaprovisions.com
Duck, venison, frozen lobster meat, game fowl, whole cleaned pigs, bushels of clams and even caribou! They also carry a full line of spices, frozen food and canned goods. Don't let the wholesale appearance of the place scare you off.

Lake George Camping Equipment

Lakeshore Drive, Bolton Landing, NY   518-644-9941
How to enjoy the Lake George islands without a boat? Call Captain Wayne Smith for boat rentals or to catch a water taxi. He will ferry you, your guests and equipment to a Lake George island for the day, or for a camping trip. To reserve an island campsite, go to www.reserveamerica.com.

Oscar's Smokehouse

22 Raymond Lane, Warrensburg, NY 12885   518-623-3431
www.oscarssmokedmeats.com
Cheese, and meats smoked on the premises for over 50 years. Gift baskets delivered anywhere.

Rain or Shine Tent Company

184 Lake Avenue, Saratoga, NY 12866   518-587-8755
www.rainorshinetent.com
Tents are their specialty, but they also rent tables and chairs.

Red Fox Books

28 Ridge Street, Glens Falls, NY 12801   518-793-5352
www.redfoxbookstore.com
Great source for books by regional writers. My favorite place for fashionable reading glasses. Friendly owners Susan and Naftaly will gladly order anything they don't carry. Support independent booksellers!

Sokol's Market

340 Aviation Road, Queensbury, NY 12804   518-792-3777
Baker Mary Ellen makes great mini butter knot rolls. They carry Boar's Head deli meats. Free grocery delivery. Call for details.

Sterling & Company

203 Glen Street, Glens Falls, NY 12801   518-745-6808
www.shopsterlingandco.com
Owners Christina and Holly have handpicked gifts you won't find anywhere else, including heirloom quality French pottery.

The Ice Man

Hudson Falls, NY 12839   518-747-5221
Custom ice sculptures by Chef Charles Jones, winner of national ice sculpting contests.

Index

158

To submit comments, suggestions, or questions, please feel free to contact me at:

SJLONGO@msn.com
www.adkcookbook.com

518-798-9598

Aunt Sally's Adirondack Kitchen
P. O. Box 4223
Queensbury, NY 12804

To place an order:

Enclose a check made out to Sally Longo in the amount of $30.00 for each cookbook ordered plus $5.00 for shipping. Orders of three or more books will receive free shipping.

Include a shipping address along with a telephone number or an email address as a way to contact you in the event there are any questions about your order.

Please allow 2 weeks for delivery.

THANK YOU!